BLUEPRINT FOR SUCCESS

BUILDING A LIFE OF DISCIPLINED PURPOSE

Major Amit Agarwal

ISBN
Paperback 979-8-89632-438-6
Hardcase 979-8-89673-422-2

A note from Amit...

My life journey has been one of transformation, adaptation, and above all, discipline. As an ex-Army officer, I was shaped by an environment where structure, focus, resilience, and adaptability were not just encouraged but expected. The leadership lessons learned during my time in the Indian Army have served as a solid foundation for everything I've done since. But I quickly realized that discipline and purpose are not qualitics confined to the military; they are essential for success in all walks of life, particularly in the fast-paced, ever-evolving corporate world.

For more than 25 years, I worked in HR leadership roles across large corporations, medium-sized enterprises, and startups. During that time, I had the privilege of working with some remarkable leaders, each with their own vision, challenges, and goals. However, I often saw a gap in the ability to turn vision into action—an inability to structure their lives and businesses with disciplined purpose.

As I transitioned from corporate life into my current career as an Executive Coach, Leadership Trainer, OD Consultant, and now as an Author, I reflect on my own journey and the powerful role discipline has played in my achievements. Over the years, I have come to realize that true leadership and sustainable success depend on creating systems of accountability, developing the right habits, and making deliberate, purpose-driven decisions.

This book, *Blueprint for Success: Building a Life of Disciplined Purpose*, is my attempt to distil the lessons I've learned throughout my career into a guide that can help others find focus and accomplishment. The strategies and methods in these pages are grounded in real-world experiences—from the military and corporate world—designed to help aspiring leaders, entrepreneurs, and professionals at all stages of their journey. This book is not merely a guide; it is a blueprint for those who want to lead with clarity, structure, and effectiveness. Whether you are an aspiring leader, an entrepreneur, or someone simply seeking self-improvement, the strategies here are designed to help you achieve your fullest potential.

Discipline is not just about following rules; it's about structuring your life in such a way that you can consistently perform at your best, regardless of the challenges you face. In this book, I have shared the tools and frameworks that have worked for me and for the individuals I've coached, and trained, showing you how to bring more structure and focus into your daily life.

Every chapter is designed to inspire you to make immediate, practical changes, whether you're looking to level up your career, build a more disciplined business, or simply become the best version of yourself. My goal is to empower you to build a life of disciplined purpose that is fulfilling, impactful, and sustainable. I hope this book will serve as a catalyst for your personal and professional growth, enabling you to make meaningful progress toward the life and career you envision.

Ultimately, I want you to understand that living with disciplined purpose is not just a goal but a way of being. It's a mindset that will enable you to navigate challenges, seize opportunities, and ultimately design a life that's both meaningful and successful.

Thank you for trusting me to guide you through this journey. I hope this book will be the spark that sets you on your own path to greatness.

Contents

Introduction

Building a Life of Disciplined Purpose

The world is constantly changing, often at a pace that leaves us feeling unanchored. In our pursuit of personal success, growth, and impact, we might achieve some milestones, but the journey can often feel chaotic and unfocused. This book, *Blueprint for Success: Building a Life of Disciplined Purpose*, offers a guide to building a life that is not only structured but also meaningfully aligned with one's deeper purpose.

The idea of disciplined purpose is simple yet profound. Discipline provides the structure necessary to turn ambitions into tangible outcomes, while purpose gives each action a deeper character. It's about creating a life where your goals and values work in harmony, allowing you to achieve more with intention and focus.

In a world that rewards quick success, discipline may seem like an outdated concept. But discipline is what transforms potential into progress. It is the anchor that keeps you aligned with your goals amid distractions, temptations, and the busyness of everyday life. Discipline provides you with a compass and a framework to bring your purpose to life consistently, despite obstacles and setbacks.

Similarly, the purpose is the **"why"** behind everything you do. When aligned with a clear sense of purpose, discipline becomes easier and more achievable. Each action does not feel like a chore but more like a step in a journey worth taking. This book shows you how to establish and maintain that purpose, linking it to every goal, habit, and endeavour so that your daily life reflects a deliberate, meaningful progression toward a life of impact.

Throughout these pages, we will explore practical strategies and real-world stories to bring these ideas to life. You'll read about leaders and innovators who have shaped their journeys with disciplined purpose, applying focus and intention to make a lasting difference. From time-tested goal-setting techniques to insights on mastering your mindset, each chapter is designed to help you cultivate a foundation of discipline that strengthens over time.

Living with a disciplined purpose isn't about perfection; it's about commitment. It's about waking up every day with clarity on what matters most and structuring your actions to reflect that clarity. By following this blueprint, you'll learn how to turn wandering aspirations into focused achievements and how to bring a sense of structure and intention to every aspect of your life.

This book invites you to embark on a journey of personal transformation. Together, we'll explore how to blend discipline and purpose into a cohesive strategy for a life that not only reaches personal milestones but also leaves a positive legacy. As you dive into each chapter, allow yourself to absorb, reflect, and, most importantly, act. This is your invitation to create a life of disciplined purpose—one deliberate step at a time.

Prologue

In the early morning haze of a remote village in Northeast India, a young 23-year-old Army officer crouched with his platoon, alert to every sound in the dense jungle around him. At the time, insurgency in the region was at its peak, requiring swift and precise action. The mission was to intercept a group of insurgents believed to be hiding in a secluded area. As the officer led his platoon through rain-soaked terrain, he knew that every decision, every step, required an unwavering focus and iron discipline.

Discipline was ingrained in his every thought and movement; a lifeline instilled in every soldier through rigorous training and countless hours of practice. He moved carefully, feeling the crunch of damp leaves beneath his boots, the weight of responsibility heavy on his young shoulders. His mind, sharpened through months of preparation, was entirely focused on the task. Ahead, in the fog of false dawn, he could see the faint glimmer of the insurgents' hideout. His senses were heightened, yet his movements were calm and deliberate. He signalled his men to halt, assured of immediate compliance, knowing that discipline in this tense moment was what bound them together.

As the team crept closer to the identified insurgent hideout and approached, tension crackled through the air like static electricity. The young officer signalled his platoon to hold, steadying his breathing and readying himself for the next few moments. He knew the slightest mistake could unravel their careful approach. Finally, he gave a silent command, and within seconds, a well-orchestrated sequence of movements unfolded. His men moved with clockwork precision, each knowing exactly what to do without hesitation. Shots rang out, but the soldiers held their ground, staying focused on the task.

As the smoke cleared, they regrouped, having successfully neutralized the threat. In the chaos, it was discipline that held the team together, that brought them to a successful accomplishment of mission without a single casualty. Standing amidst the smoke and clearing mist, the officer felt the profound weight of this truth: discipline was more than following orders; it was a shared commitment, an unspoken bond that fortified them in the face of danger. This was what set them apart, what made them a cohesive, undefeatable force.

Years later, having transitioned from the military to a corporate career, the former officer found himself navigating an entirely different kind of battleground. Now a Chief Human Resource Officer at a high-growth company, he faced new challenges that came not from insurgents or hostile terrain but from internal politics, rapid scaling, and fierce market competition. In his new world, the battles weren't fought with weapons but with decisions, policies, and the relentless pressure to deliver. Yet, just as in the Army, people looked to him for guidance and resilience.

During one particularly high-stakes project—a complex merger that threatened to destabilize the organization—he found himself once again relying on the discipline that had been his foundation. Departments clashed, egos flared, and timelines pressed relentlessly forward. He saw the cracks forming as teams became divided, each pushing for their agenda. In a tense meeting, with voices raised and tempers frayed, he remembered the discipline he had carried from the Army: the ability to step back, focus on the broader objective, and bring people together under a shared purpose.

He took a deep breath, drawing from the calm he had once found amidst the chaos of the jungle. He called for order and began guiding the room with a sense of discipline and purpose that steadied his colleagues. He reminded them of the mission they were collectively working toward, instilling the same clarity and unity he had once fostered in his platoon. As the weeks wore on, he structured their work with precision, just as he had in his Army days, creating an environment where each person understood their role and contribution. The merger, once at risk of collapsing under conflicting interests, proceeded smoothly. Just as in the Army, discipline allowed him to achieve clarity amidst chaos, grounding the team and driving them to a successful outcome.

Reflecting on both these experiences, he realized that discipline was not just a skill for the battlefield; it was a way of life, an essential force that shaped both individual character and collective success. Whether in the heat of a jungle or the intensity of a corporate boardroom, discipline enabled him to lead with purpose, resilience, and strength. He knew that, whether leading troops or steering a business, discipline was the common denominator for success. This book is his blueprint, crafted from a lifetime of lessons, to help readers build a life anchored in disciplined purpose, navigating every challenge with focus and fortitude.

Discipline is the Bridge Between Dreams and Reality

It has the Power to turn Fleeting Ambition into Enduring Success

Chapter 1

Disciplined Purpose

The concept of **"Disciplined Purpose"** isn't just about being productive, focused, or goal-oriented—it is a deeper alignment of your inner drive with deliberate, sustainable actions that guide your life toward fulfilment. It's about creating a roadmap for your life and having the discipline to stick to it, no matter how many distractions or challenges arise. This disciplined approach helps you build not just a career or a business, but a life of meaning and impact.

For entrepreneurs and aspiring leaders, the idea of purpose is paramount. It goes beyond a job description or the pursuit of wealth. Purpose is the foundation that keeps you grounded in moments of uncertainty and the driving force that fuels you during tough times. Discipline is not about mindlessly following routines, but about sticking to values and systems that align with your long-term vision. When united, purpose and discipline form an unbeatable bond—a foundation that allows you to persevere and thrive, even in the face of adversity.

Disciplined purpose involves a commitment to intentional, well-thought-out actions and consistent efforts to achieve long-term success. However, it's not just about hard work; it's about channelling energy with focus and aligning your actions with meaningful, clear objectives. Disciplined purpose becomes the foundation for growth, ensuring that every step taken is purposeful and contributes to their overarching mission.

Let's look at Howard Schultz's transformation of Starbucks. His disciplined focus on creating a community-driven brand, guided by a clear purpose of "human connection over coffee," allowed Starbucks to expand beyond just selling coffee; it created a global experience. Schultz's journey wasn't free from hurdles, but his commitment to a larger, meaningful purpose helped him navigate them successfully.

The concept of Disciplined Purpose is therefore not merely theoretical; it requires practical application. As you continue on your path to success, reflect on how your daily choices reflect your deeper purpose. Each decision should serve as an opportunity to reinforce that purpose, ensuring that even in the face of challenges, you maintain a course of action that aligns with your true aspirations.

A disciplined purpose means remaining vigilant about your "why." It's about reminding yourself consistently of why you are doing what you do, and using that as the compass when making critical decisions.

1. The Power of Purpose: A North Star

The power of purpose serves as the guiding principle that shapes every decision, action, and strategy in your life. It acts as a North Star—a fixed point of reference that remains constant, no matter how turbulent the journey may become. When you have a clearly defined purpose, it gives your life and career direction, making it easier to weather distractions, challenges, and setbacks. This unwavering and untiring sense of purpose helps you focus on the long-term vision, ensuring that every decision aligns with your core values and ultimate objectives.

Elon Musk's vision for space exploration and sustainable energy isn't just a business venture—it's a guiding force that influences the entire culture of companies like SpaceX and Tesla. His purpose of advancing human life on Mars or fighting climate change through electric vehicles is the driving factor behind every innovation, every business decision, and every risk taken. Musk's success lies in his unwavering commitment to this greater purpose, which in turn fuels his leadership and the work ethic of his teams.

In the entrepreneurial realm, disciplined purpose becomes a powerful differentiator. Without a clear purpose, business ventures risk losing momentum, succumbing to the immediate pressure of the market, or short-term gains. A purpose-driven business isn't swayed by fleeting trends; instead, it maintains its focus, making strategic decisions that support a lasting legacy.

Moreover, purpose is intrinsically linked to motivation and resilience. When the going gets tough, as it inevitably will, the strength of your purpose can help you push forward. It creates a sense of urgency and importance, reminding you why you started in the first place. This constant reaffirmation of your why fuels perseverance, even when the path is unclear.

The power of purpose is, therefore, more than just a concept; it's the foundation of sustained success, personal fulfilment, and organizational growth. Like a North Star, it keeps you on course when everything else seems to be in flux. By establishing a strong, purposeful vision and staying aligned with it, you create a resilient blueprint for achieving long-term goals.

2. Disciplined Action: The Bridge Between Vision and Reality

Vision is the spark, but disciplined action is the fuel that keeps it burning. A compelling vision, no matter how powerful, remains abstract unless it's backed by consistent, purposeful action. It is through disciplined action that you translate dreams into tangible outcomes. Without this action, even the most brilliant ideas can remain nothing more than unrealized potential.

Steve Jobs's vision of creating beautifully designed technology that was intuitive and user-friendly was clear, but it was his disciplined, relentless pursuit of that vision; constant iteration, setting rigorous standards, and an unwavering commitment to quality, that brought his vision to life. Every product release, and every technological advancement, was a result of this disciplined action that spanned years of hard work and investment.

This connection between vision and action is what differentiates successful leaders from dreamers. Disciplined action is about consistency and intentionality. It's not about sporadic bursts of effort; rather, it's the ability to show up day after day and do what needs to be done to stay committed to the long-term goal. For entrepreneurs building businesses, this might mean developing systems, setting clear daily goals, and sticking to routines that help sustain their progress.

Another important aspect of Discipline in Action is also the ability to stay adaptable while staying true to your vision. Even with a clear goal, the journey is rarely linear. Obstacles, changes in market conditions, and unforeseen challenges will inevitably arise. Disciplined action is the ability to respond to these changes without losing sight of your purpose. It's the practice of continuously re-evaluating your methods, improving your strategies, and maintaining flexibility while still marching forward with commitment.

In personal transformation, disciplined action means developing daily habits that align with your ultimate goals. Consider yourself working toward health and fitness. You might set a clear vision of improved well-being, but the daily commitment to eating healthy, exercising, and prioritizing rest is what converts that vision into physical transformation. You would inevitably face challenges; family commitments to be fulfilled, professional deadlines to be met, and so on. However, Disciplined Action is about staying consistent, even when motivation ebbs or challenges arise.

Ultimately, disciplined action is the engine that drives vision forward. It is the practical, tangible step that makes dreams a reality. Leaders who understand this cultivate the ability to act consistently with purpose and create legacies that endure. Whether it's in business, personal growth, or any other domain, disciplined action is the bridge that connects where you are now to where you want to be.

3. The Role of Environment in Supporting Purpose and Discipline

Environment plays a pivotal role in fostering both purpose and discipline. Whether we are aware of it or not, the people, surroundings, and tools we engage with daily have a profound effect on shaping our mindset and behaviour. For leaders striving to create a life of disciplined purpose, a supportive environment is not a luxury, it is essential.

Serena Williams is a prime example of how the environment plays a pivotal role in fostering purpose and discipline. Growing up in Compton, California, she faced challenges but also benefited from an environment carefully shaped by her father, Richard Williams. He saw potential in her and her sister Venus, creating a rigorous yet supportive atmosphere for them to excel in tennis. Serena's purpose was ignited early by her father's belief that she could become one of the greatest athletes. This clear purpose provided her with a vision to pursue greatness. Her environment reinforced discipline through relentless training sessions, structured routines, and a focus on resilience, even in adverse conditions.

Despite limited resources initially, her father's encouragement and the high standards he set turned her environment into a launchpad for greatness. As her career evolved, she surrounded herself with coaches, teammates, and mentors who nurtured her purpose and reinforced her discipline, ultimately leading her to dominate the world of tennis.

A supportive environment isn't just about physical surroundings—it's about the social ecosystem you create. The people around you must align with your values and vision. When you have individuals who challenge you, encourage you, and hold you accountable, the pursuit of a disciplined purpose becomes a shared journey rather than a solitary one. Just as a student may be inspired by their teacher or a team excels under a passionate leader, so can a positive environment push individuals to greater heights.

Similarly, having a structured, purpose-driven **space** is vital for staying focused. This can include your workspace, your daily rituals, or even your digital environment. Creating a distraction-free workspace, whether that's a clean desk or a clear inbox, removes distractions from the path to progress. When you consistently choose environments that facilitate focus and creativity, your daily actions align with your goals without having to exert constant willpower.

The role of the environment also extends to the tools and resources at your disposal. These tools should not just be functional but should reinforce your vision. Whether it's investing in a reliable project management system, choosing books and podcasts that align with your growth goals, or investing in a fitness tracker to keep you accountable to your health regimen, your environment can serve as an omnipresent reminder of your discipline and purpose.

But perhaps the most critical aspect of the environment is the support system—those who help you maintain your discipline. Whether it's a business partner, a coach, or a **mastermind group***, having individuals who check in with you, give constructive feedback, and offer encouragement can provide the external motivation you need on days when your inner drive wanes.

> **A Mastermind Group is a small, focused community of like-minded individuals who regularly share ideas, provide mutual support, and collaborate on achieving personal or professional goals. The concept, popularized by Napoleon Hill in his book Think and Grow Rich, emphasizes collective intelligence, where the combined knowledge, experiences, and perspectives of the group enhance individual growth and success.*

The role of the environment is, therefore, not passive. It's a dynamic force that interacts with your internal world of purpose and discipline. A carefully curated environment—both social and physical—ensures that you're continuously supported, that distractions are minimized, and that every choice you make is aligned with your greater vision.

Optimize Your Physical Environment for Focus and Creativity

Your physical surroundings significantly influence your ability to concentrate and innovate.

- ***Declutter for Clarity:*** *A clutter-free workspace reduces distractions. Ensure your desk is organized with only the essentials to keep your mind focused.*

- ***Personalize Your Space:*** *Include items that inspire you, such as motivational quotes, artwork, or photos, but avoid overloading the space. A balanced approach promotes creativity without overwhelming the senses.*
- ***Lighting Matters:*** *Natural light boosts productivity and creativity. If unavailable, use warm, adjustable lighting to create a comfortable and inviting workspace.*
- ***Ergonomics for Comfort:*** *Invest in a chair, desk, and tools that support proper posture to minimize discomfort and fatigue and help you maintain focus for extended periods.*
- ***Incorporate Nature:*** *Adding plants or natural elements can reduce stress and stimulate creative thinking. Research shows that greenery enhances cognitive performance.*

Create Rituals That Support Productivity and Inspiration

Rituals anchor your day and set the tone for focus and creativity.

- ***Morning Rituals:*** *Start your day with activities like journaling, reading, or exercise to prime your mind for focus.*
- ***Dedicated Time Blocks:*** *Allocate specific times for deep work and creative thinking, using techniques like the Pomodoro Method to maintain focus.*

- ***Reflection and Downtime:*** *Reserve time at the end of the day for reflection. Reviewing successes and areas of improvement strengthens focus and encourages creative problem-solving.*

4. The Integration of Self-Discipline and Compassion

In the pursuit of disciplined purpose, self-discipline, and compassion are often seen as opposing forces. Self-discipline is about control, focus, and execution, while compassion is associated with understanding, kindness, and emotional connection. However, when integrated effectively, they form a powerful dynamic that leads to not only personal success but also sustainable well-being and leadership.

At the core of this integration lies the concept that *self-discipline is not just about rigidly following rules or routines, but about making intentional choices that lead to long-term growth.* It's about pushing past resistance and doing the hard work necessary to achieve goals, but also knowing when to pivot, adjust, and *show compassion towards oneself during moments of struggle.* Compassion, in this sense, is not a weakness, but an important aspect of maintaining emotional resilience and perseverance.

Tim Cook, Apple's CEO has often spoken about the importance of mental health and well-being for his team, encouraging a culture of empathy and support at Apple. He recognizes that to be highly disciplined in the workplace, employees need to feel seen and supported, particularly when facing personal or professional challenges. His leadership illustrates how self-discipline can be balanced with compassion for others' struggles, creating a more sustainable, harmonious work environment.

Similarly, compassion for oneself is a critical part of building and maintaining self-discipline. Entrepreneurs and Leaders, especially, often face overwhelming challenges, yet those who practice compassion don't beat themselves up when setbacks occur. Instead, they show grace toward their shortcomings, learn from them, and refocus their efforts with renewed commitment. Richard Branson has always been candid about the many times he's failed, but his ability to show self-compassion, rather than self-criticism, has enabled him to bounce back stronger. His willingness to be kind to himself when things go wrong allows him to stay disciplined and focused on his long-term goals.

When combined, discipline and compassion create a balanced approach to leadership and personal success. Compassion allows you to recognize that setbacks, mistakes, and challenges are part of the journey—natural aspects of life that help you grow, evolve, and develop greater resilience. *Discipline, then, becomes more effective when it is rooted in a healthy relationship with yourself.* You don't need to punish yourself for mistakes; instead, you can refocus your energy and motivation in a way that fosters growth without guilt.

In practice, this would look like giving yourself time to rest and recharge without guilt after a period of intense productivity. It could also involve setting boundaries with others, recognizing when to say no, and allowing time for self-reflection and emotional recovery. Leaders who integrate self-discipline and compassion not only achieve personal success but also inspire their teams to do the same, creating a culture of both performance and empathy.

Ultimately, self-discipline without compassion can lead to burnout and a sense of isolation, while compassion without discipline can result in a lack of direction, motivation, or achievement. But when both are integrated, you create a sustainable foundation for pursuing your goals with vigour, while remaining connected to your inner self and the people around you. This holistic approach ensures that the pursuit of purpose doesn't come at the expense of emotional health or the well-being of those you lead.

5. The Discipline to Keep Evolving

The discipline to keep evolving is the cornerstone of lasting success. It is not enough to simply set goals and achieve them; the true measure of growth lies in the ability to continuously evolve in response to changing circumstances, new learning, and personal growth. This requires a mindset of adaptive discipline, where you are committed not only to what you are doing today but to improving your approach tomorrow, if required, and to making course corrections.

I. Continuous Learning as a Discipline

In an ever-changing world, leaders must commit to lifelong learning. The discipline to keep evolving means intentionally creating growth opportunities—whether it's reading, attending seminars, or engaging with mentors. Satya Nadella, CEO of Microsoft, exemplifies this discipline through his commitment to continuous learning and fostering a growth mindset within his organization. Nadella's approach to leadership transformation at Microsoft was not static; it required ongoing education and adaptation, both for himself and his team. His ability to shift from a traditional, more rigid management style to one that embraces agility and learning is a powerful testament to the discipline of evolution.

II. Embracing Change with Purpose

To stay relevant and effective, evolution must be purposeful. This means setting aside time to reflect on your goals and progress, and then recalibrating when necessary. Adi Ignatius, the editor-in-chief of Harvard Business Review (HBR). joined HBR in

2009. At the time, the magazine was grappling with declining print readership and the rapid shift to digital media. The traditional business model was under pressure, and many publications were struggling to adapt to the digital age. Ignatius embraced the challenge with a clear purpose: to modernize HBR while maintaining its reputation as the gold standard of business thought leadership. He sought to make the publication more accessible, relevant, and innovative for a global audience. Ignatius spearheaded a digital transformation by launching HBR.org, creating an app, and diversifying content with podcasts, videos, and interactive tools. Under his guidance, HBR shifted to a subscription model that blended high-quality print with a strong digital presence, ensuring the publication's financial sustainability and continued influence. This demonstrates that even leaders of niche organizations can embrace change to navigate disruption, proving that purpose-driven adaptability is critical for success at every level.

III. Being Comfortable with Discomfort

The discipline to evolve often means stepping out of your comfort zone. Change is uncomfortable, and as leaders, we need to recognize that growth requires discomfort. A significant part of this evolution involves embracing failures as feedback. The discipline to keep evolving includes the willingness to make mistakes, learn from them, and push forward. Jeff Bezos, in Amazon's early years, made several bold moves, some of which didn't initially pay off. Yet, he always maintained a forward-focused mindset, adapting, experimenting, and refining his strategy.

6. The Role of Feedback and Self-reflection

To evolve effectively, self-discipline is essential, but it must be balanced with feedback and reflection. Continually seeking input from others, whether from mentors, peers, or your team, allows for a more accurate understanding of your progress and areas for growth. Oprah Winfrey has often credited her growth to the mentors and feedback she has received along the way. This disciplined openness to feedback has allowed her to pivot in her career and embrace new challenges, even when the world thought she had already achieved it all.

The discipline to keep evolving, therefore, is about maintaining momentum, staying curious, and being willing to adapt. It's a commitment to lifelong learning and growth, an ability to pivot when necessary, and the resilience to embrace discomfort. True success is not static—it requires ongoing evolution, a disciplined approach to continuous improvement, and the courage to change when the situation demands it. This approach ensures that you don't just achieve success once, but sustain and build upon it for a lifetime.

Defining and living a life of disciplined purpose requires a shift in perspective—one that acknowledges the importance of both purpose and discipline and the relationship between the two. It is not enough to simply have a purpose; you must be disciplined enough to work towards it every day. Equally, it is not enough to be disciplined; your discipline must be guided by a purpose that provides meaning to your actions.

Ultimately, a disciplined life with a clear purpose is about achieving both personal and professional success in a sustainable and fulfilling way. It's about knowing where you're going, creating the systems and habits that support that journey, and staying grounded even when the path gets tough. *The power of disciplined purpose lies not in the destination, but in the journey itself,* one where every step is intentional, and every action aligned with the greater vision you have for your life.

Without Discipline, even the Grandest Plans

Remain a mere Whisper of Possibility!

Chapter 2

Building Blocks of Discipline

In a world constantly shifting with new trends, distractions, and demands, discipline is often the missing ingredient separating aspiration from achievement. Discipline is more than a single quality; it's a complex, multilayered structure that enables people to overcome momentary impulses in favour of long-term goals. For aspiring leaders, entrepreneurs, and anyone seeking personal transformation, understanding the building blocks of discipline can lay a solid foundation for lasting success.

At its core, discipline is a skill. Like any skill, it can be refined, enhanced, and mastered over time. However, building discipline doesn't come from sheer willpower alone. It requires a deep understanding of key components that work together to create a resilient mindset capable of withstanding challenges. In this chapter, we'll unpack these building blocks, exploring real-world examples to illustrate how these principles manifest in real lives and businesses. By doing so, we can gain insight into what makes discipline a powerful force for change and growth.

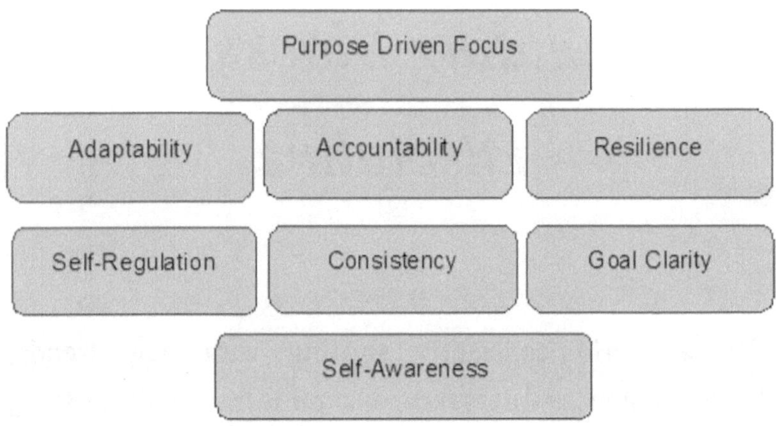

**The building blocks of Discipline*

1. Self-Awareness: The Starting Point of Discipline

Every journey toward discipline starts with self-awareness. *It's the practice of understanding your strengths, limitations, triggers, and motivations*. Without self-awareness, discipline can feel like an endless battle against unknown forces, but with it, discipline becomes a strategic game.

Self-awareness enables you to recognize why certain goals matter to you and what habits are holding you back. In practical terms, building self-awareness involves regular reflection and honest self-assessment. Take time each week to evaluate your actions and their alignment with your values and goals. **Journaling*** is a powerful tool to help organize your thoughts, track your progress, and bring awareness to any emerging patterns in your behaviour. By understanding the root causes of your actions, you can tailor your discipline to work with your natural tendencies rather than fighting against them.

To build deeper self-awareness, actively explore your inner thoughts, emotions, and responses to daily situations. This can be done through regular introspection, mindfulness practices, and setting aside time to reflect on experiences, particularly challenging ones. Another effective approach is to seek out diverse feedback, especially from people who observe you in different contexts. Tools like journaling, meditation, and personality assessments (such as Myers-Briggs or Thomas Profiling) can further reveal your core motivations, values, and behavioural patterns, helping you understand how they align with your goals.

Additionally, observing your reactions under stress and in unfamiliar environments offers valuable insights into both your natural tendencies and areas for growth. Over time, this awareness strengthens decision-making and emotional resilience, allowing you to respond more effectively to both challenges and opportunities.

Journaling *is the practice of regularly writing down thoughts, feelings, and experiences in a notebook, diary, or digital format. It is a tool for self-reflection, personal growth, and emotional well-being. Journaling can be used for various purposes, including managing stress, boosting creativity, tracking progress toward goals, or simply organizing thoughts.*

How to Get Started with Journaling

- ***Choose Your Medium:*** *Decide whether you prefer a notebook or a digital app.*
- ***Set a Schedule:*** *Aim to journal daily or a few times a week, even for just 5–10 minutes.*
- ***Create a Comfortable Environment:*** *Find a quiet space where you can write without distractions.*
- ***Be Honest and Open:*** *Write authentically without fear of judgment. This is your private space.*
- ***Use Prompts:*** *Prompts like "What made me happy today?" or "What challenges did I face?" can help you get started.*
- ***Stay Consistent:*** *Over time, journaling becomes a habit that integrates naturally into your routine.*

Journaling is highly flexible, and there's no "right" way to do it. The key is to make it meaningful and beneficial for your personal or professional journey.

2. Goal Clarity: Knowing Your True North

Once self-awareness is established, the next building block of discipline is having a clear vision or purpose. Discipline without direction is a wasted effort; it's like sprinting full speed without knowing where you're going. True discipline arises when you're deeply connected to your goals.

Setting clear, specific, and meaningful goals provides a sense of direction, enabling disciplined action to feel purposeful. Kiran Mazumdar-Shaw is the founder of Biocon, a Biotechnology Company, based in Bangalore, India. Her goal - to establish a leading biotech company in India, despite the odds, gave her the clarity and motivation to persevere through years of challenges. Her vision didn't just keep her going; it also aligned her daily actions, helping her make decisions rooted in her mission rather than reacting impulsively to external pressures.

To develop goal clarity, consider using tools like **vision boards*** or written goal statements. Write down your goals in specific terms and revisit them regularly to ensure they still align with your evolving vision. This process not only keeps you grounded but also adds layers of meaning to your disciplined actions, helping you stay committed even when faced with adversity. To clarify your goals, start by envisioning your ideal future. Break down big objectives into smaller, actionable steps that keep you consistently moving forward. Additionally, revisit and adjust your goals regularly to ensure they remain relevant and aligned with both your inner purpose and external circumstances. This approach not only provides direction but also builds motivation, resilience, and discipline as you journey toward a fulfilling life.

> **A* ***Vision Board*** *is a visual representation of your goals, dreams, and aspirations. It's typically a collage of images, words, and symbols that reflect what you want to achieve or experience in life. Vision boards are used as a motivational tool to help clarify, concentrate, and maintain focus on specific life goals. Vision boards rely on the principles of visualization and goal-setting. Regularly seeing your goals keeps them top-of-mind, it primes your brain to notice opportunities aligned with your aspirations. This fosters a belief in your ability to achieve your dreams.*

3. Consistency: The Power of Habit

Consistency, often described as the backbone of discipline, unlocks the power of habit by entrenching behaviours into our routines until they become second nature. Consistency is the glue that binds disciplined actions together over time. Without consistency, even the most carefully laid plans can falter. The discipline to keep showing up, day after day, is often what separates those who achieve their goals from those who fall short. The small actions we repeat daily ultimately shape our identity, influence our outcomes, and transform goals into achievements.

The Japanese manufacturing giant Toyota's dedication to consistency in quality and efficiency is foundational to its success. Known for its "kaizen" philosophy, Toyota focuses on continuous improvement by implementing disciplined processes that are followed consistently at every level. This approach, while requiring significant effort, creates a stable framework for disciplined action that benefits both employees and customers.

To build consistency, start by establishing clear, attainable micro-habits that align with your larger goals. Practice patience and prioritize progress over perfection. Over time, each repeated effort builds momentum and reinforces your commitment, creating a reliable foundation for long-term growth and success. Developing consistency can start small. Establishing a routine, setting achievable daily goals, and tracking progress can create a sense of accomplishment that reinforces the habit. Starting with small wins, such as a daily exercise or reading routine, builds confidence and resilience. Once consistency is ingrained, larger goals feel more achievable, and discipline becomes second nature.

To maintain consistency, design an environment that supports your habits, such as setting visual reminders, removing distractions, or linking new behaviours to established routines. Tracking progress is also beneficial—it provides measurable motivation and helps identify what strategies work best for you. Remember, consistency is not about rigid discipline; it's about showing up persistently with intention.

4. Self-Regulation: Mastering Impulse Control

Self-regulation is the discipline of controlling impulses, especially in challenging situations, and is a cornerstone of effective discipline. Self-regulation is particularly crucial in high-stress environments where the temptation to react impulsively is heightened. Mastering impulse control involves recognizing and managing immediate desires or distractions to focus on long-term goals. This skill allows us to respond thoughtfully rather than react impulsively, enhancing productivity and decision-making.

To build self-regulation, start by identifying triggers and emotional cues that lead to impulsive actions. Practicing mindfulness helps here, allowing you to pause and assess your feelings without judgment. Additionally, using techniques like **"if-then"** planning, can redirect impulses into productive actions. For example, "If I feel the urge to check social media, then I'll take a short walk instead".

Another powerful tool is setting specific boundaries to structure your environment in ways that reduce temptations. For instance, putting your phone away during focused work periods or working in spaces where distractions are minimal can foster better self-control. Also, gradually increasing the challenges in tasks (like extending your focused work time) can strengthen your impulse resistance.

Reflection is equally crucial. Tracking and analysing instances of impulsive versus controlled behaviour provides insights into patterns and progress. Over time, this awareness sharpens your ability to act in alignment with goals rather than momentary desires, ultimately building resilience and fostering a disciplined mindset.

When Satya Nadella took the helm as CEO, he faced intense scrutiny and pressure to improve the company's direction. Rather than reacting impulsively to criticism, Nadella practiced self-regulation, taking time to listen, learn, and reflect. His measured approach helped foster a collaborative culture, turning Microsoft into a more innovative, disciplined organization.

Practicing self-regulation can be challenging, especially when facing emotional triggers. Techniques such as mindfulness, deep breathing exercises, or even a short pause before responding can help manage reactions and promote thoughtful decision-making. Self-regulation isn't about denying emotions but rather about acknowledging them and choosing a response that aligns with your goals.

5. Resilience: Staying the Course Through Adversity

Resilience is the quality that keeps us grounded and moving forward, even when challenges threaten to derail us. Building resilience is about developing a mindset and practices that allow you to bounce back, learn from setbacks, and keep pursuing your goals. One of the first steps is reframing adversity as a learning opportunity rather than a roadblock. *When faced with failure or unexpected hurdles, resilient individuals analyse the experience, identify lessons, and make adjustments to their approach without being discouraged.*

A strong sense of purpose also fuels resilience. When you have a clear understanding of your "**why**"—the deeper reasons behind your efforts—it's easier to persevere through tough times. This purpose acts as a guiding light, reminding you of the end goal even when the journey becomes challenging.

Ritesh Agarwal, the founder of OYO Rooms faced numerous setbacks as he expanded his budget hotel chain. However, his resilience enabled him to pivot, learn from failures, and keep pushing forward. His disciplined approach to problem-solving allowed him to build OYO into a well-recognized brand globally.

Self-care practices, such as maintaining physical health, mental breaks, and mindfulness, also strengthen resilience. These habits build mental and physical endurance, giving you the energy to cope with stress. Social support is equally valuable; connecting with mentors, friends, and colleagues provides perspective, encouragement, and insights that help you regain focus when things seem overwhelming.

Developing resilience involves reframing setbacks as opportunities for growth. Reflect on past challenges and identify the lessons learned. When facing a current obstacle, remind yourself of your strengths and previous successes.

This mindset shift not only strengthens discipline but also builds a positive outlook that encourages perseverance. Resilience ultimately requires a mix of self-belief and adaptability. Trusting in your capabilities, accepting change, and maintaining flexible strategies enable you to stay the course, reinforcing discipline and ensuring that obstacles are met with determination rather than defeat.

6. Accountability: Holding Yourself Responsible

Accountability is a powerful driver of self-discipline, pushing us to hold ourselves responsible for our goals, actions, and results. Building accountability starts with setting clear, specific goals and deadlines. When you define exactly what you want to achieve, it's easier to measure your progress and identify areas where you may need to improve.

Regular self-assessment is another critical component. Periodically checking in on your progress keeps you aligned with your objectives and helps you recognize any lapses in discipline. This involves honestly evaluating where you are, acknowledging both your achievements and setbacks, and planning actionable steps to overcome obstacles. In the corporate world, accountability is often structured through performance reviews and goal-setting frameworks, like OKRs (Objectives and Key Results). At Google, and many other Organizations I know of, employees are encouraged to set ambitious goals (stretch goals) and hold themselves accountable for achieving them. This culture of accountability drives a disciplined approach to work and encourages employees to take ownership of their progress.

Another way to strengthen accountability is by sharing your goals with a mentor, coach, or accountability partner who can provide honest feedback and support. Knowing that someone else is aware of your objectives can increase your motivation and commitment, as it introduces an external element of accountability. In addition to external support, tools like journaling, setting reminders, and using apps to track your habits can reinforce accountability on a daily basis. These tools provide a tangible record of your commitment, offering clarity on your progress and areas that may need more attention.

Embracing accountability means accepting responsibility for your results, whether positive or negative. This mindset promotes growth by encouraging you to learn from your experiences rather than blaming external factors.

7. Adaptability: Adjusting with Purpose

Adaptability is an essential skill in today's rapidly changing world, requiring leaders to not only react to change but also to adjust their approach with intention and purpose. Discipline doesn't mean rigidly sticking to a plan at all costs; rather, it involves having the flexibility to adapt without losing sight of your purpose. This mindset involves being open to learning, experimenting with new strategies, and actively seeking feedback on performance. Building adaptability starts with self-awareness, recognizing both strengths and blind spots in one's approach to change. When leaders are attuned to their responses and their team's needs, they can pivot quickly without sacrificing alignment with core goals.

Another key to adaptability is a willingness to embrace a growth mindset, a concept highlighted by psychologist **Carol Dweck**. A growth mindset frames challenges as opportunities for growth, rather than threats to success. Leaders who cultivate this mindset encourage their teams to learn from mistakes, approach obstacles with curiosity, and stay engaged with shifting objectives. This fosters a culture of resilience, where employees are motivated to develop new skills and seek creative solutions.

In practice, adaptability also demands a balance between flexibility and structure. Leaders need to know when to adjust plans without compromising their vision or core values. During times of economic instability, adaptive leaders may shift priorities, redirecting resources to high-impact areas, while still upholding the organization's overall mission and standards.

Practicing adaptability involves being open to feedback, evaluating results, and remaining flexible in your approach. Regularly assessing your progress and adjusting your strategies accordingly allows for growth and prevents burnout. Adaptability ensures that discipline remains relevant in changing circumstances, reinforcing a sustainable path to success. Ultimately, adaptability involves continuous improvement, cultivating both an openness to change and a disciplined commitment to growth.

8. Purpose-Driven Focus: The Ultimate Foundation

Purpose-driven focus is perhaps the most crucial building block of discipline. It is Infact, the core foundation of disciplined success. It's about aligning every decision, action, and habit with a clear, meaningful purpose—often termed one's **"True North."** This foundation serves as a compass, helping leaders and individuals navigate the complexities and distractions of daily life, ensuring that their energy is directed toward what genuinely matters. When discipline is tied to a meaningful purpose, it no longer feels like a burden but rather a pathway to fulfilment.

When the focus is purpose-driven, it becomes resilient, helping individuals push through challenges without veering off course. Rather than scattering their efforts across numerous goals, purpose-driven individuals commit to a concentrated, singular vision. This focus enhances clarity, filtering out distractions and increasing productivity.

Fostering purpose-driven focus within a team can inspire others to work with a deeper commitment. It encourages people to look beyond immediate tasks, considering how their work contributes to larger organizational or societal goals.

Building this foundation requires regular self-reflection to remain aligned with core values. Leaders can deepen purpose-driven focus by clarifying their goals, examining their motivations, and adjusting strategies to stay aligned with their larger vision. This foundation supports lasting fulfilment and the consistent achievement of long-term goals, ultimately creating a disciplined life driven by impact and meaning rather than short-term rewards or approval.

Understanding the building blocks of discipline is like constructing a blueprint for your success. Self-awareness, goal clarity, consistency, self-regulation, resilience, accountability, adaptability, and purpose-driven focus, each play a distinct role in creating a disciplined mindset. As you cultivate these qualities, discipline becomes less about force and more about flow - an integrated part of who you are.

Building a disciplined life is a lifelong journey. By grounding your actions in these principles, you lay the foundation for personal excellence and purpose-driven success. Whether in business, relationships, or personal growth, these building blocks will serve as reliable pillars that support your aspirations, helping you not only achieve your goals but to do so with integrity and resilience. In this way, discipline becomes not just a tool but a transformative practice that enriches every aspect of life.

True freedom is found in the consistency of discipline, not the chaos of indulgence

Chapter 3

Your Purpose

For discipline to take root in our lives, it must be anchored in a deep sense of purpose. Without purpose, discipline becomes mechanical, rigid, and ultimately unsustainable. Purpose drives us; it fuels the fire that keeps us going even when the road gets rough. It's the reason behind our actions, the force that propels us toward achieving the life we want. Without a clearly defined purpose, we risk falling into the trap of aimless effort and short-lived bursts of willpower that fizzle out when the going gets tough.

Purpose, however, is not something you can simply read about and adopt on the spot. It's a discovery - a journey of self-exploration that, when undertaken with sincerity, reveals the deepest truths of what you are truly passionate about. Finding your purpose is the foundation on which all forms of discipline, success, and personal fulfilment are built. It aligns your efforts and directs your energy in the most meaningful way.

1. The Search for Purpose: A Universal Journey

Across cultures and histories, people have sought to discover meaning and purpose. It's what has led to the creation of religions, philosophies, and even scientific breakthroughs. It is, in essence, the driving force of humanity's greatest achievements. It is a deeply human pursuit, shaped by the desire to make a meaningful impact and to feel connected to something larger than oneself. Throughout history, purpose-driven individuals have left indelible marks on their industries, communities, and the world.

The reality is, that identifying your purpose requires both introspection and action. It's not enough to simply sit back and hope that it will "find" you. You have to engage actively with your inner self and the world around you to discover it.

The quest for purpose is not confined to the extraordinary. It is a journey that every individual, from aspiring leaders to entrepreneurs, must undertake. In fact, the process of finding purpose is often the catalyst for personal transformation. For many, it begins with self-reflection and the alignment of personal values with professional endeavours. Identifying one's purpose requires a deep understanding of one's motivations, strengths, and long-term aspirations.

Arianna Huffington is the co-founder of The Huffington Post. Huffington has shifted her focus to promoting well-being and health through her company, Thrive Global. After experiencing burnout herself, her purpose now lies in helping people prevent burnout and lead more balanced, fulfilling lives. She is a prime example of someone who evolved her career to align with her personal purpose.

Oprah Winfrey's career journey is a story of finding purpose through service and connection. With a media empire that spans television, books, and online platforms, Oprah's purpose has always been to inspire and empower others. She famously turned her struggles and challenges into a platform for people to share their stories, lifting others along the way.

These examples highlight the role that purpose plays not only in personal success but also in fostering broader societal impact. Purpose fuels perseverance through challenges and becomes the backbone of great leadership, guiding decision-making and influencing organizational direction. For leaders, understanding this sense of purpose is essential to their ability to inspire and lead their teams effectively.

When people find and embrace their purpose, they often experience a profound transformation. Purpose is more than just a career goal or a business objective; it's a moral compass that influences how one lives, works, and interacts with the world. This alignment between purpose and action leads to greater fulfilment, sustained energy, and a sense of direction.

However, the journey to purpose is rarely linear. It involves exploring multiple avenues, confronting fears, and making adjustments. The search for purpose is dynamic, it may evolve as one's circumstances and perspectives change. A successful entrepreneur who initially built a business to achieve financial independence may later discover that their true purpose is to solve a pressing social problem. This shift is common and speaks of the fluid nature of purpose.

The search for purpose is an essential part of the human experience, particularly for leaders and entrepreneurs. It serves as a guiding force that propels individuals forward, even in the face of adversity. Whether it is through creating impactful products, leading transformative companies, or giving back to communities, purpose shapes the trajectory of one's life and legacy. For those striving for personal excellence, embracing a clear sense of purpose can turn ambition into meaningful achievement, creating lasting change in both professional and personal realms.

2. Understanding the Role of Purpose in Discipline

Once you have a clear sense of purpose, discipline becomes an ally, not an obstacle. When the goals you are working toward are intrinsically meaningful to you, the disciplined actions you take every day don't feel like a chore. Instead, they feel like an essential part of your journey. The truth is, when people work toward a meaningful goal, they will find a way to push through challenges, setbacks, and resistance. When the purpose is clear, you are not simply doing something for the sake of doing it—you are creating something bigger than yourself.

Purpose is the cornerstone of discipline. Without a clear sense of purpose, maintaining focus and consistency becomes a struggle, as there is no compelling reason to stay committed to long-term goals. Discipline flourishes on a deeper motivation that fuels persistence, even when challenges arise. When an individual understands their purpose, every action aligns with their larger goals, making discipline more than just a routine—it becomes a pathway to fulfilling a greater vision.

Imagine a successful entrepreneur who is driven by the purpose of creating innovative solutions for sustainability. This sense of purpose not only keeps them disciplined in their work but also encourages them to remain resolute through failures and setbacks. In this way, purpose acts as a stabilizing force, guiding decisions and actions.

In leadership, a clear sense of purpose helps to set a framework for discipline, not only for individuals but for entire teams or organizations. Leaders who communicate their purpose effectively motivate their teams to stay disciplined, knowing that their work is contributing to something meaningful. This alignment between purpose and discipline fosters a sense of ownership and accountability, enabling leaders to inspire sustained effort and excellence.

> *Discipline, then, is not about rigid adherence to rules or self-imposed restrictions, but about making intentional choices that align with a larger purpose. As one becomes more attuned to their purpose, discipline no longer feels like a burden—it becomes an essential tool for navigating the journey toward meaningful achievement.*

3. The Challenges of Finding Purpose

While the concept of **"Purpose"** may seem straightforward, many people struggle with it. In our fast-paced world, we are bombarded by so many competing interests, distractions, and pressures that it's easy to lose sight of what truly matters. Our culture often values external success - money, fame, status - without giving adequate attention to internal fulfilment and purpose. This can leave individuals feeling unfulfilled, disconnected, and aimless, even if they have reached high levels of success in their careers or personal lives.

For entrepreneurs, this challenge is particularly acute. The demands of building a business, especially one that is successful and sustainable, can make it hard to distinguish between what is urgent and what is important. In the early stages of building a business, it's easy to focus only on growth metrics, customer acquisition, and other operational tasks, neglecting the deeper purpose behind the business. However, businesses that thrive in the long term are those whose founders have a well-defined purpose and integrate that purpose into every aspect of their operations.

The key is to take the time to reflect and ask yourself:

Why am I doing this? Is this truly in alignment with my values and aspirations? Is it serving something larger than just personal gain?

These aren't always easy questions to answer, but they are essential for identifying your true purpose.

4. Identify Your Purpose

I. *Reflect on Your Values*

The first step in discovering your purpose is to clarify your values. What do you stand for? What principles guide your decisions? This could involve anything from social responsibility to personal integrity, creativity, or family. Understanding your values provides the foundation for everything you will do moving forward. If your actions are not aligned with your core values, you will always feel a sense of inner dissonance, which will eventually undermine your discipline.

II. *Look for Patterns in Your Life*

Often, your purpose is hidden in the patterns of your life. Think about the moments in your past when you felt most fulfilled or excited. What were you doing? Who were you with? Often, these experiences point to the activities or causes that give you the deepest sense of satisfaction and meaning. Your purpose is usually linked to those moments of joy and fulfilment, not just external rewards or accolades.

III. *Consider Your Strengths and Skills*

Your purpose often lies at the intersection of what you are good at and what you are passionate about. What are your strengths? What comes naturally to you? Often, the things that you excel at are clues to your purpose. So, if you love solving complex problems, your purpose may be related to innovation or entrepreneurship. If you excel at nurturing and coaching others, your purpose may lie in leadership or mentorship.

IV. *Ask Yourself the Big Questions*

To go deeper into your purpose, ask yourself some big life questions. These might include: What do I want my legacy to be? How do I want to impact the world? What do I want my work to mean to others? While these questions can feel overwhelming, they often reveal the core of your purpose. The key is not to rush the process.

It takes time, self-reflection, and patience to discover your true calling.

V. *Test Your Purpose Through Action*

Once you've identified your purpose, the next step is to take action. *Purpose is not just about thinking and reflecting—it's about doing.* Start small, experiment, and see what resonates with you. If your purpose is to help others live healthier lives, for instance, start by volunteering at a health organization or creating content around wellness. Your purpose will become clearer as you align your actions with your aspirations.

VI. *Aligning Purpose with Discipline*

Once you have clarity around your purpose, the next step is aligning your daily actions with that purpose. This is where discipline comes in. Without discipline, your purpose remains an abstract idea, something you think about but never fully live out. The disciplined pursuit of your purpose means aligning your everyday choices—how you manage your time, how you approach your work, and how you engage with others—with your ultimate vision.

Purpose without discipline can lead to wasted potential. Similarly, discipline without purpose can feel hollow and exhausting. It's the integration of the two that leads to sustainable success and fulfilment. A startup founder may be incredibly disciplined about their daily routine, but without a purpose-driven mission, they may find themselves burnt out or overwhelmed by the relentless pursuit of goals that don't align with their true calling.

Aligning purpose with discipline is about creating a cohesive connection between what drives you and how you structure your actions. When you have a deep understanding of your purpose, discipline becomes a natural extension of your goals. It helps you stay focused, especially during difficult times, because you are consistently reminded of the bigger picture. So, let's say, if your purpose is to make a significant impact in education, then discipline in your daily tasks—whether it's continuous learning or dedicated time to teach—becomes a clear choice that aligns with your mission, rather than a set of chores you are compelled to do. This alignment strengthens resilience, fosters consistency, and ensures that your daily actions contribute to long-term success.

The relationship between purpose and discipline is symbiotic. Purpose provides the clarity and direction necessary to sustain discipline, while discipline ensures that you stay committed to your purpose. By identifying your purpose and using it as a guide, you can cultivate the kind of discipline that leads to meaningful, lasting success.

Ultimately, your purpose is what will keep you going when external rewards are scarce, when obstacles seem insurmountable, and when you feel like giving up. It will be the anchor that holds you steady during the storms of life and business. With that kind of purpose-driven discipline, you will build a life of lasting impact, fulfilment, and success.

Discipline isn't a punishment;

it's the tool that chisels away at mediocrity to reveal excellence

Chapter 4

Designing Purposeful Routines

One of the most pivotal decisions an aspiring leader or entrepreneur can make is designing a purposeful routine. Many people I know think that success is achieved through grand, epic shifts in life, but almost always, it is the consistent, deliberate actions taken every day that shape the future. The small habits we cultivate every day, our routines, are the foundation upon which we build our dreams, goals, and long-term achievements.

In today's world, where distractions are a dime a dozen, and external pressures seem never-ending, a well-thought-out routine can offer clarity, focus, and a sense of control. But building a disciplined routine is not just about filling the day with tasks, it's about consciously deciding how to use your time in alignment with your deepest values and purpose. Purposeful routines are those that, when designed carefully, help you move closer to the person you want to be and the success you aspire to create. But how do you go about designing such routines? Let's explore this in greater detail.

1. The Power of Routine

First, let's understand the power of routine. Routines are the structure within which we operate daily. The more mindful and intentional our routines, the more likely we are to develop behaviours that support our long-term goals. Successful people don't just wake up to a day full of tasks; they wake up to a day that has been deliberately designed for their success. At first glance, it may seem mundane - a daily set of tasks to get through - but its true power lies in the predictability and discipline it fosters. When we commit to routines, we aren't just filling our time with tasks; we're creating a structure that supports long-term success.

I. *Psychological Benefits of Routine*

Humans are creatures of habit. Psychological research highlights that routines play a vital role in conserving mental energy and enhancing decision-making. A key study published in the *Journal of Personality and Social Psychology* discusses how decision fatigue - the mental depletion from making multiple choices - can reduce self-control over time. By automating repetitive tasks through routines, individuals can reserve mental energy for more complex or significant decisions. Decisions, big or small, demand cognitive resources. Every time you choose what to wear, what to eat, or when to work out, you're using up valuable mental energy. A routine eliminates the need for these decisions, freeing up your brainpower for more important matters—like problem-solving and strategic thinking.

Moreover, routines create a sense of predictability and control, which can reduce stress and anxiety. Structured daily rhythms help minimize uncertainty, leading to a calming effect on the mind. This aligns with findings from Tel Aviv University, which emphasize how predictable patterns in life contribute to better emotional regulation and cognitive efficiency. Sachin Tendulkar followed a strict schedule all through his career, starting with a morning workout, followed by practice, and ending his day with reflection and relaxation. This consistent routine helped him not only stay physically fit but also mentally sharp for the challenges ahead, ensuring that his focus was on performance and not on what to do next.

In practical terms, routines also streamline daily actions, improve focus, and even enhance sleep quality by establishing consistent habits like regular bedtimes and mealtimes. These benefits not only support mental clarity but also foster an environment conducive to creativity and personal growth

II. *Routine as a Key to Self-Discipline*

Self-discipline is often cited as the key to success, but how do we build it? A disciplined individual doesn't rely on willpower alone. Instead, they create an environment and a routine that makes staying disciplined easier. Willpower can be fleeting, especially when it's tested by distractions, stress, or lack of motivation. Routine, on the other hand, creates a framework where self-discipline becomes a habit.

Routines create **habit loops**, a concept popularized by *Charles Duhigg in The Power of Habit.* These loops consist of three components: cue, routine, and reward. Consistent routines, such as starting the day with a workout or journaling session, reinforce positive behaviours and build discipline over time. The brain recognizes the reward associated with a routine, making it easier to maintain discipline even when motivation wanes. The work of psychologist *Roy Baumeister* on willpower suggests that habits alleviate the strain on self-control, making it easier to sustain disciplined actions.

III. *The Consistency Factor*

Routine builds consistency. Consistency is the cornerstone of achievement in any field, from business to sports to personal development. I have noticed many successful leaders use time-blocking—a technique that segments their day into focused, undistracted periods. This method allows them to dedicate specific time to high-priority work, ensuring that no task gets overlooked.

Routines also help foster the idea of compound progress. Compound Progress refers to the exponential growth achieved through small, consistent efforts over time. Similar to compound interest in finance, it builds on itself as incremental improvements accumulate, leading to substantial results. This principle applies in various fields, such as skill development, fitness, or productivity, where persistence turns minor gains into major successes. The key lies in consistency and patience, as early results may seem negligible but grow significantly with time and effort. Think about how daily exercise routines add up over weeks, months, and years, gradually building endurance and strength. In the business world, routines like consistently reviewing key performance indicators, improving processes, or checking in with the team help create sustainable progress over time. It's about small, incremental changes, compounded over time, leading to monumental growth. Routines make growth predictable, as long as they are purposeful and aligned with a larger goal.

IV. *Flexibility Within Routine*

While the power of routine lies in its consistency, it's also important to allow for flexibility within your schedule. The idea isn't to follow a rigid script but to maintain the discipline to adjust as needed. This flexibility helps you respond to new opportunities or challenges while staying aligned with your long-term goals. Life is unpredictable, and strict routines may not account for sudden changes, like emergencies or creative bursts of energy. A flexible routine builds buffers or contingencies, allowing room to adjust without guilt or disruption. So, if a morning workout isn't possible, a flexible routine may include options for an evening session or a lighter activity like stretching.

Imagine how, many top CEOs manage their schedules. While they might follow a routine in terms of time-blocking their meetings, emails, and strategic work, they remain adaptable. If an urgent issue arises, their ability to shift gears and prioritize becomes essential. This blend of structure and flexibility is what makes routines powerful in the face of life's unpredictable nature.

A rigid schedule can also feel monotonous over time, potentially reducing motivation. Flexibility allows variety, such as experimenting with different work settings or trying new activities. Working at a desk, a café, or a park can invigorate creativity and focus. Flexibility also encourages self-compassion by recognizing that not every day will go as planned. Flexibility within routine ensures that discipline and adaptability coexist, creating a foundation for sustainable progress, creativity, and well-being. This balance supports mental health and a long-term consistency.

V. *The Emotional Anchor of Routine*

Routines can also serve as emotional anchors. In times of uncertainty or stress, having a predictable routine can bring a sense of calm and control, which can help foster resilience during challenging times. For individuals, who often face high-pressure situations, routine provides stability. When you're not sure how to approach the chaos of a busy day or are feeling overwhelmed, knowing exactly what's next on your agenda can help lower anxiety and provide a sense of control. Routines help anchor habits that contribute to emotional health, such as regular exercise, mindfulness practices, or quality time with loved ones. These repeated actions become touchpoints that enhance mood and foster a sense of accomplishment.

Routines don't just organize your day; they offer emotional stability, enhance resilience, and help you navigate life's challenges with greater composure and well-being. By grounding you in familiar and comforting patterns, they become pillars of emotional strength.

2. Building a Routine That Works for You

Not all routines are created equal. The key to building a routine that works for you is customization. You must design your daily schedule in a way that serves your goals, your personal rhythm, and your energy levels. Are you an early riser? Are you most productive after lunch or in the evening? Recognizing your natural rhythms is crucial in crafting a routine that you can stick to.

So, for an entrepreneur developing a routine, blocking time for deep work, brainstorming, and creative thinking, and then separating time for operational work or team management would probably work best. The mix will depend on the demands of their business as well as their personal peak performance times.

I. *Building Your Routine: Start With Purpose*

The first step in designing a purposeful routine is to understand what truly matters to you. When you are clear about your values, goals, and priorities, you can then design your day to reflect them. The most successful routines are rooted in a deep sense of purpose. They don't just aim at checking off tasks; they focus on aligning those tasks with your larger mission in life.

For entrepreneurs building businesses, this means taking the time to structure your day so that your efforts are directed at things that will lead to growth. Prioritize tasks that will help you scale your business or improve your leadership skills. Don't waste your time on tasks that don't align with your long-term vision.

Similarly, as an aspiring leader, it's crucial to identify the key activities that will help you grow as a leader. For instance, set time aside in your routine for reading books on leadership, practicing self-reflection, or engaging in discussions with mentors or peers. These activities are investments in yourself, and the consistency of doing them daily or weekly is what pays off in the long term.

II. **Time Blocking***: *Structure Is Key*

When you start building a purposeful routine, the structure becomes your best ally. A significant method to ensure you stay disciplined is time-blocking. This method involves dividing your day into blocks of time where you focus on one task or activity. Time-blocking not only helps in being organized but also prevents procrastination and ensures that you make the most of your available time.

In the book ***Deep Work, author Cal Newport*** **discusses the concept of "deep work"**, the ability to focus without distraction on a cognitively demanding task. Newport argues that in a world full of distractions, deep work has become increasingly rare, making it more valuable. If you want to achieve great things in your business or leadership journey, you need to prioritize this type of focused, uninterrupted work. Time-blocking is one of the best ways to ensure that you are making time for deep work and focusing on your most important tasks.

For entrepreneurs, this might mean blocking off time for product development, business strategy, or client outreach. For leaders, it could involve setting time aside for team meetings, one-on-one coaching sessions, or strategic thinking. By establishing a consistent and structured schedule, you set yourself up for focused action and prevent time from slipping away without making significant progress.

> ***Time Blocking*** *is a productivity method where you allocate specific blocks of time to particular tasks or activities in your schedule. Instead of working through a general to-do list, you assign each task a time slot, ensuring focused attention and reduced multitasking. This method helps manage priorities, limit distractions, and improve time efficiency. By setting boundaries for tasks, it also creates space for deep work and rest periods. Tools like calendars or apps can be used to organize these blocks, enabling better control over daily and long-term goals.*

3. Establishing Rituals: The Art of Discipline

Rituals are intentional, symbolic actions performed regularly that hold deeper meaning beyond mere functionality. Unlike habits, which become automated behaviours, rituals are purposeful and often carry an emotional or psychological significance. They are powerful tools for fostering discipline, creating a sense of control, and aligning actions with values and goals. Rituals often carry symbolic weight, reinforcing discipline by connecting actions to personal values or goals. Athletes, like tennis star Rafael Nadal, follow meticulous pre-game rituals to channel focus and mental readiness. These rituals symbolize a commitment to performance excellence.

Rituals Infact serve as cues that signal a shift in mindset or activity, making transitions smoother and more deliberate. For instance, some people Light a candle before starting creative work which signals the beginning of focused effort, while a nightly ritual like reading, signals winding down for rest. The stability provided by rituals can be a source of emotional strength. During stressful periods, rituals help reinforce a sense of normalcy and calm, fostering resilience.

Studies in behavioural psychology show that rituals enhance performance and emotional regulation by reducing anxiety and creating a sense of control. For instance, a study in the *Journal of Psychological Science* demonstrated that pre-task rituals improve focus and outcomes in stressful situations. Establishing rituals transforms ordinary routines into purposeful practices, fostering discipline and emotional well-being. By infusing everyday actions with intention and meaning, rituals provide a structured yet flexible framework for achieving goals, navigating transitions, and finding fulfilment in the process.

4. The Role of Reflection: Course-Correcting as You Go

A key element of a purposeful routine is the ability to reflect on your actions. Without reflection, routines become mechanical, and you risk losing sight of the bigger picture. Reflection helps you course-correct and fine-tune your routine as you go. After all, you are a dynamic individual with evolving goals, so your routine should be flexible enough to adapt to those changes.

Reflection plays an essential role in maintaining discipline and growth by allowing you to course-correct as you move forward. The act of reflection is like a mental checkpoint, where you assess your actions, identify patterns, and adjust your strategies. This process is not just about evaluating whether you've met your goals, but understanding how your habits, routines, and decisions align with your purpose.

Ray Dalio, founder of Bridgewater Associates, attributes much of his success to regular reflection and feedback. Dalio believes that systematically reflecting on decisions, both successful and failed, enables learning and improvement. He even institutionalized this practice within his organization through the use of "**reflection journals***," a tool that helps his team analyse what went right or wrong in various projects, encouraging continuous improvement.

> ***Reflection Journal** is a personal writing tool used to record thoughts, experiences, and emotions to promote self-awareness and growth. Unlike regular diaries, these journals emphasize introspection and analysis, encouraging you to draw insights and identify patterns in your behaviour or decisions. Commonly used in personal development, education, and professional settings, they help clarify goals, track progress, and process challenges. Writing regularly in a reflection journal enhances critical thinking, emotional regulation, and problem-solving skills. It is a structured yet flexible practice that fosters both personal and professional growth.*

Reflection doesn't need to be overly complex. It could mean taking a few moments at the end of each day to jot down what worked, what didn't, and why. Weekly or monthly reflections allow for a deeper assessment, helping you to recognize emerging patterns and make any necessary course corrections. Consistent reflection helps to prevent the "drifting effect" in which small, seemingly insignificant deviations from your plan compound over time and lead you off course.

In practice, the power of reflection can be magnified by focusing on specific areas such as time management, productivity, relationships, and emotional well-being. For example, if your goal is to increase productivity, reflect on the tasks that drained your energy versus those that boosted it. This can help you make better decisions about where to allocate your time and energy in the future.

Lastly, it's crucial to view reflection as a judgment-free exercise. Rather than critiquing yourself harshly, approach it with curiosity and openness. This mindset fosters resilience, encouraging you to make positive changes without the burden of guilt or frustration. As you refine your approach through regular reflection, you build an adaptable framework that supports disciplined growth, allowing you to stay aligned with your purpose and respond to challenges with agility and insight.

5. The Power of Discipline in Creating Momentum

One of the most rewarding aspects of a well-designed, disciplined routine is the momentum it creates. Momentum is a force that propels you forward, even when you hit obstacles. At its core, momentum is the cumulative force built from consistent actions, where each step forward generates the energy and confidence to take the next. The process begins with setting small, achievable goals, which create a sense of accomplishment and build intrinsic motivation. This sense of progress fuels an upward cycle: each success makes it easier to stay committed to the next task, leading to more substantial accomplishments over time.

Consider the journey of an athlete in training. Early sessions might seem small and insignificant, yet the discipline of showing up daily allows for gradual improvement. This consistency compounds—physical stamina builds, skills sharpen, and confidence grows. The same principle applies to any field of pursuit: by committing to disciplined actions, even in the face of challenges or setbacks, we can sustain forward motion and overcome inertia.

A great example of this can be found in the story of Amul, one of India's most successful dairy companies. Amul's success is not just due to its products but also its disciplined marketing and consistent innovation. Over the decades, Amul has stayed true to its core values while adapting to changing consumer preferences. Their commitment to consistent quality, disciplined operations, and innovative, consistent marketing has given them an edge in a highly competitive market.

Momentum also grows when discipline is paired with a strong purpose or vision. Knowing why you're taking specific actions adds a layer of emotional motivation, turning routine actions into powerful steps aligned with a larger goal. A business leader, who practices daily discipline in refining their communication or decision-making skills will not only improve personally but will influence their organization's momentum. As their actions inspire others, this collective energy propels the company forward.

To maintain momentum, it's also essential to recognize milestones along the way, celebrating small wins to reinforce commitment. Each milestone boosts morale, and recognizing it serves as a reminder of progress, fostering a sense of achievement that further fuels discipline. When setbacks occur, the habit of discipline acts as a safeguard, helping to prevent demotivation and allowing you to quickly regain momentum.

Discipline fuels momentum by transforming consistent effort into exponential progress, helping you stay on course, maintain energy, and reach larger goals with a sense of purpose. Discipline in your routine will create momentum that will carry you through tough times. This consistency of focused, deliberate action will help you weather challenges and keep you on course toward your objectives.

Designing a purposeful routine isn't just about filling your day with tasks; it's about aligning your actions with your deeper purpose and ensuring that every activity contributes to your overall goals. Your routine is a direct reflection of your discipline and your commitment to success. By being intentional with your time, using time-blocking to structure your day, incorporating rituals for mental clarity, and reflecting on your progress regularly, you set yourself up for long-term achievement.

Discipline isn't something that's forced, rather it's something that becomes a natural part of your life. Likewise, your routines can serve as the foundation for your success. Design them with purpose, stick to them with discipline, and over time, you'll see the results compound into a life of meaning, purpose, and excellence.

Purpose is the compass that guides you through the storms of uncertainty

Chapter 5

Building Resilience

In the journey of personal transformation and disciplined growth, setbacks are inevitable. They can arise from missed goals, external challenges, unforeseen crises, or even personal misjudgments. For those who strive for a disciplined purpose—whether aspiring leaders, entrepreneurs, young professionals, or individuals on a structured self-improvement path, developing resilience is critical. Resilience isn't merely about bouncing back; it's about learning, adapting, and moving forward with renewed focus. Building resilience is a skill set that can be cultivated, refined, and strengthened, and it is what separates those who merely endure from those who learn and grow.

In this Chapter, we dive into the invaluable skill of **resilience**—a core attribute for anyone navigating the complex journey of personal and professional growth.

Resilience, in essence, is the capacity to adapt and recover when faced with adversity or unforeseen challenges. It's not just about surviving difficult times but learning to succeed amid setbacks, cultivating the mental and emotional strength that fuels long-term success.

Building resilience requires a proactive mindset and strategic approaches. It is essential to understand that setbacks, rather than being detours from our goals, can offer rich learning experiences, shaping us into more adaptable and disciplined individuals. Embracing setbacks as growth opportunities can strengthen one's discipline and commitment to purpose, enabling us to maintain a clear focus even during periods of hardship.

In practical terms, *resilience-building is about developing tools and habits that allow us to respond rather than react to stress.* This includes cultivating emotional awareness, nurturing a growth mindset, and, crucially, understanding the power of consistent self-reflection. Ultimately, resilience is the foundation that supports sustained personal growth. By harnessing discipline to navigate challenges with strength and flexibility, we build a life not only of purpose but of profound inner resilience.

1. Understanding Resilience: More than Bouncing Back

Resilience involves an active process of growth and transformation. It's the discipline to face adversity head-on, maintain emotional stability, and keep progressing. In a world that constantly demands adaptation, resilience becomes the anchor. The Japanese concept of kintsugi, the art of repairing broken pottery with gold lacquer, highlights the cracks rather than hiding them. In many ways, resilience is our mental kintsugi, allowing us to emerge stronger, and showing the beauty in having overcome adversity.

Understanding resilience as "more than just bouncing back" involves viewing it as a process of personal evolution and transformation rather than mere recovery. True resilience reshapes our perspective on challenges, encouraging us to see setbacks not as deterrents but as critical learning experiences that refine our abilities and reinforce our resolve.

While bouncing back is an aspect of resilience, it doesn't capture the full depth of what it means to be resilient. At its core, resilience is about learning and adapting. It's about examining each setback and understanding what went wrong, what factors were within our control, what weren't and what lessons we can learn from these. Instead of simply returning to a previous state, resilience involves emerging stronger, with new insights and a renewed commitment to our goals.

This concept can be illustrated through stories of accomplished leaders who didn't just recover from failures but used them as stepping stones. Entrepreneurs who face business downturns and come out with a refined business model or individuals who overcome personal hardships and develop a profound sense of empathy and purpose illustrate resilience as an ongoing journey of personal and professional growth.

Real resilience requires developing both inner strength and practical coping mechanisms. An essential part of building resilience is having a solid foundation of discipline that helps sustain focus and mental clarity when setbacks occur.

1. Embracing Setbacks as Stepping Stones

Resilience is fundamentally a mindset—a belief that setbacks are opportunities to learn and grow. This mindset requires viewing failures or disappointments not as dead-ends but as stepping stones to greater understanding and success. Embracing setbacks as stepping stones means transforming each challenge or failure into an opportunity for growth. This approach requires reframing setbacks not as endings but as essential, often transformative, parts of a larger journey. Rather than seeing them as barriers, setbacks can be viewed as opportunities for reflection, adaptation, and skill enhancement, ultimately leading to greater resilience and wisdom.

> *To use setbacks positively, it's essential to assess each experience with objectivity, asking questions like: What went wrong? How could I approach this differently? What strengths did I discover within myself during this setback?*

Consider the late Ratan Tata, Chairman Emeritus of Tata Group, who spearheaded Tata Motors' acquisition of Jaguar Land Rover (JLR). Initially, this acquisition faced major challenges, including market downturns and cultural integration issues. However, Tata's disciplined approach to resilience—focusing on long-term value and investing in revamping JLR's operations and branding—turned a struggling brand into one of Tata's most successful global assets. This resilience was not blind optimism; it was a strategic acceptance of challenges, making adjustments, and learning from missteps. Viewing setbacks as stepping stones fosters a learning-oriented resilience and enables purposeful adaptation.

Setbacks offer a chance to uncover and leverage strengths we may not have realized. This includes building emotional resilience, sharpening problem-solving abilities, or becoming more adaptable. Every setback, if approached with curiosity and determination, teaches invaluable lessons about perseverance, flexibility, and perspective. By adopting this mindset, we can turn even the most challenging moments into experiences that build character, deepen our skills, and bring us closer to our goals.

2. Building Emotional Fortitude through Self-Awareness

Resilience is closely tied to emotional intelligence and the ability to manage one's emotions under pressure. This emotional fortitude allows you to remain calm, make informed decisions, and inspire confidence in others during difficult times.

Emotional resilience starts with self-awareness—the discipline of recognizing one's emotional triggers and developing healthy coping mechanisms. Building emotional fortitude through self-awareness is about developing a deeper understanding of your emotions, strengths, and triggers. This process begins with introspection, which helps individuals recognize patterns in how they react to challenges or stress. Self-awareness enables you to approach setbacks with a balanced perspective, rather than being overwhelmed by immediate emotional responses.

When we pause to examine our feelings, we begin to identify underlying beliefs and fears that may be affecting our reactions. For instance, a failure at work might initially feel like a personal shortcoming, but through self-reflection, it becomes clear that this fear stems from a need for validation. By recognizing this, we gain control over how to manage that fear, rather than letting it dictate our actions.

Self-awareness also involves understanding your strengths and limitations. This is essential for resilience, as it builds confidence in what you bring to the table and a realistic perspective on what might require further development. For example, understanding that you have a strong ability to stay calm under pressure can reinforce your confidence in high-stress situations, while acknowledging that you may need to work on assertiveness can focus your efforts constructively.

Practices such as journaling, mindfulness, or seeking feedback from trusted peers can foster this awareness. Each of these tools provides a platform for observing thoughts and emotions without immediate judgment. Through these practices, individuals develop an internal compass that helps them navigate challenges with clarity, patience, and a deeper understanding of their resilience. Reflecting on experiences, particularly challenging ones, helps gain insights into personal reactions, enabling a more measured response in the future.

3. Developing a Problem-Solving Mindset

A core component of resilience is a problem-solving mindset—the ability to analyse situations objectively and generate actionable solutions. Instead of succumbing to setbacks, resilient individuals discipline themselves to break down problems into manageable parts and address each part systematically. Developing a problem-solving mindset is about cultivating a proactive and solution-oriented approach to challenges. This mindset encourages us to see obstacles as opportunities for growth rather than insurmountable roadblocks. Adopting this perspective requires mental flexibility, resilience, and creativity, as well as a structured approach to addressing issues.

One key step is reframing problems to make them manageable. Instead of viewing a situation as a personal failure, it helps to break it down analytically: What factors led to this problem? What aspects are within my control? By examining these details, we avoid becoming overwhelmed and can begin identifying actionable steps.

Another vital part of a problem-solving mindset is embracing curiosity. Individuals with this trait ask questions like, "What can I learn from this?" and "Are there alternative solutions I haven't explored?" This openness allows us to find unique solutions that may not have been immediately apparent. An entrepreneur facing market changes, for instance, might pivot their product offering, discovering new business opportunities as a result.

In one of the Organizations, I consulted; while there were multiple business lines, there was more focus on one. This business line contributed to 60% of revenues and 55% customer base. Due to market dynamics when this business line tanked, the organization was in a fix, losing its main revenue stream, slowly but surely. However, we were quickly able to shift focus to other, existing business lines, create new revenue streams, restructure the organization, stay afloat, and grow from there.

Resilience plays a central role, since often, setbacks require multiple attempts to resolve. Building the mental fortitude to handle repeated failures without giving up is critical. It's also essential to remain adaptable, recognizing when a strategy needs adjustment rather than stubbornly sticking to a single approach.

Root Cause Analysis (RCA)

Root Cause Analysis involves several structured steps to identify and address the underlying reasons for a problem. Here's a step-by-step guide:

1. *Define the Problem: Clearly articulate the issue, focusing on the specifics of what happened, where, and when. Use measurable terms where possible. Example: Instead of saying "System crashed," specify "The server crashed at 3 PM, affecting X users."*

2. *Gather Data: Collect all relevant data and evidence related to the problem, such as logs, reports, interviews, or direct observations. This ensures an accurate understanding of the context and contributing factors.*

3. *Identify Possible Causes: Brainstorm potential reasons for the problem. Tools like brainstorming sessions, Fishbone (Ishikawa) diagrams, or flowcharts can help visualize contributing factors.*

4. *Identify the Root Cause: Trace back to the fundamental issue that triggered the problem. The root cause is often not immediately obvious and may require combining evidence from multiple sources.*

5. *Develop Solutions: Create targeted, practical solutions that address the root cause rather than just symptoms. Focus on preventive measures to ensure the problem does not recur.*

6. *Implement and Monitor: Put the solutions into action and track their effectiveness over time. Establish clear metrics to measure success and ensure the issue is resolved permanently. Document RCA*

7. *Communicate Findings: Share the insights and lessons learned with relevant stakeholders to foster organizational improvement and prevent similar issues in the future.*

Incorporating structured problem-solving techniques - such as brainstorming, root-cause analysis, and SWOT (Strengths, Weaknesses, Opportunities, and Threats) analysis—helps bring clarity to the situation. Root-cause analysis can uncover underlying issues that may not be obvious initially, guiding you toward more sustainable solutions. Using these frameworks not only refines your problem-solving abilities but also builds confidence as you approach complex challenges methodically.

For aspiring leaders and professionals, this problem-solving mindset can be cultivated through structured thinking practices like mind mapping, the **"5 Whys" technique**, or scenario planning. These exercises, when practiced regularly, enhance resilience by equipping individuals with frameworks to approach setbacks constructively rather than emotionally.

> *The **"5 Whys" technique** is a problem-solving tool used to identify the root cause of an issue by repeatedly asking "Why?"—typically five times. Each answer forms the basis for the next question, helping to explore the cause-and-effect relationships underlying the problem. This simple, yet effective technique uncovers systemic issues and helps identify solutions that address the core problem, not just the symptoms. It's often used in quality improvement, project management, and troubleshooting scenarios. By digging deeper into the problem, the process reveals insights that can lead to better solutions.*

4. Building a Support Network

Another vital factor in building resilience is creating a support network. Resilience does not mean facing everything alone; it means knowing when and how to seek guidance, advice, or assistance. Strong networks, whether friends, mentors, colleagues, or professional communities, provide emotional support and diverse perspectives that enhance resilience.

Indra Nooyi, former CEO of PepsiCo, is known for her disciplined focus on balancing profitability with social responsibility, Nooyi relied on a robust network of mentors and advisors. This network helped her navigate tough times, from strategic pivots to public scrutiny, allowing her to stay resilient and focused on her long-term vision. For aspiring leaders, actively building a supportive network is not just about career advancement but about cultivating a well of resources that can be tapped into during challenging times.

5. Cultivating Flexibility and Adaptability

Flexibility is a cornerstone of resilience. It requires a willingness to adjust plans, modify approaches, or even change goals when circumstances shift. This adaptability must be rooted in disciplined thinking, helping leaders avoid impulsive reactions and instead make deliberate, well-considered adjustments.

In the context of the COVID-19 pandemic, countless businesses around the world had to pivot almost overnight. A prime example is Zoho Corporation, led by CEO Sridhar Vembu. With employees suddenly unable to access offices, Zoho adapted by implementing remote work practices and expanding its digital collaboration tools to maintain productivity. Vembu's disciplined approach to flexibility ensured that Zoho could weather the disruption, keep morale high, and emerge stronger. This adaptability became an organizational asset, reinforcing the company's resilience in an unpredictable landscape.

6. Physical and Mental Well-being as Resilience Foundations

Physical health plays an integral role in resilience. Exercise, nutrition, sleep, and mindfulness practices provide the physical and mental stamina needed to face setbacks with clarity and strength. Disciplined self-care is not an indulgence; it's a fundamental investment in resilience.

Leaders like Jeff Bezos have emphasized the importance of physical fitness in sustaining their energy and mental resilience. For entrepreneurs, young professionals, or anyone facing demanding situations, prioritizing regular exercise, mindfulness practices, and healthy sleep patterns are essential practices. This approach not only increases physical endurance but also improves mental agility, focus, and emotional stability, all of which are critical to resilience.

7. Creating a Long-Term Vision and Keeping It in Sight

Creating a long-term vision is essential for guiding your actions and decisions, especially during challenging times. It serves as a beacon, helping to align your daily efforts with your larger life goals. To keep this vision in sight, it's important to break it down into smaller, achievable milestones and continually evaluate your progress. Reflecting on your long-term purpose during setbacks can maintain motivation and inspire persistence. Successful leaders and entrepreneurs focus on long-term goals, despite facing significant short-term obstacles, highlighting the power of a clear, unwavering vision.

Consider the story of Dr. Devi Shetty, founder of Narayana Health in India. Driven by a vision of providing affordable healthcare, he encountered numerous challenges, from regulatory hurdles to financial constraints. However, Shetty's unwavering commitment to his mission has helped him navigate these setbacks and persevere. This long-term vision has anchored his resilience, allowing him to innovate in healthcare delivery and impact millions of lives. Keeping a vision in focus provides an essential sense of purpose, enabling individuals to maintain discipline even during turbulent times.

8. Practicing Mindfulness to Build Resilience

Practicing mindfulness is a powerful tool for building resilience because it helps you remain centred and focused, even in the face of adversity. By cultivating mindfulness, you learn to stay present and fully engaged in the moment, instead of getting overwhelmed by past mistakes or future uncertainties. This focus enables better emotional regulation, clarity of thought, and improved problem-solving skills. Leaders like Steve Jobs often credited mindfulness with helping them maintain their creativity and poise under pressure, demonstrating how it can foster resilience both in personal and professional contexts. Regular mindfulness practice can reduce stress, enhance emotional intelligence, and ultimately fortify your capacity to bounce back from setbacks.

This practice is especially evident among some of the world's most successful leaders, including the late Steve Jobs, who practiced Zen meditation to develop focus and resilience. Daily mindfulness can serve as a resilience tool, enhancing self-awareness, reducing anxiety, and improving decision-making under stress.

Building resilience against setbacks is not a one-time effort but an ongoing practice, grounded in discipline and fortified by mental agility, emotional intelligence, adaptability, and purpose. Resilience means developing skills that can be drawn upon in every sphere of life, from professional ambitions to personal challenges.

As aspiring leaders and professionals pursuing excellence, resilience becomes a way to convert obstacles into learning experiences, failures into lessons, and setbacks into stepping stones. Ultimately, the disciplined pursuit of resilience equips individuals with the strength and wisdom to navigate the complexities of life, pushing them toward a path of sustained growth and enduring success.

When you live with purpose, every struggle becomes a stepping stone, not a stumbling block

Chapter 6

Distractions and Procrastination

Let us now explore effective strategies for overcoming distractions and procrastination. By identifying the common sources of distractions, we can develop better habits that promote focus and productivity. Additionally, we will also look at practical techniques to combat procrastination and maintain motivation. Let's dive into understanding how to stay on track and achieve our goals.

In the pursuit of a disciplined, purposeful life, two of the most pervasive and destructive challenges are distractions and procrastination. These issues silently erode time, focus, and energy, preventing aspiring leaders, entrepreneurs, young professionals, and personal growth seekers from fully realizing their potential. For many, the need to conquer these obstacles isn't just about achieving success; it's about reclaiming control over their lives.

The modern world offers endless distractions—notifications, emails, social media, the 24/7 news cycle, and more; all designed to captivate our attention and lure us away from focused work. Meanwhile, procrastination, the habit of postponing essential tasks, compounds the problem, often leading to stress, poor performance, and a lack of fulfilment. The good news is that by understanding these challenges and implementing actionable strategies, anyone can regain control and maintain focus, transforming distractions and procrastination into tools for growth.

1. Understanding the Roots of Distraction

Distractions can be both internal and external. Understanding the roots of distraction involves exploring both external and internal sources that impact focus and productivity. Externally, we're surrounded by digital distractions like notifications, emails, and social media, all designed to capture attention continuously. Internally, our own emotional and cognitive processes often lead us to procrastinate or avoid tasks. Anxiety, perfectionism, or the allure of instant gratification can cause us to delay important activities in favour of simpler, immediate rewards.

Furthermore, neuroscience reveals how our brains are wired to seek novelty, which can make it difficult to resist distractions. External distractions are often easier to identify—such as social media, television, and messages. However, internal distractions are equally disruptive, often harder to recognize, and can be deeply rooted in habits, thoughts, or emotional states. Fear, insecurity, boredom, and lack of motivation are common internal distractions that, if unchecked, drive individuals to seek out mindless diversions.

Addressing these roots requires building self-awareness about why we become distracted. By recognizing specific patterns, like our tendency of turning to distractions when we feel overwhelmed or uncertain, we can create targeted strategies to manage them. Techniques like mindfulness, prioritization, and environment control can help, as well as develop healthier habits around technology and social interactions. Think about a young entrepreneur striving to establish their business. They may feel overwhelmed by the magnitude of their goals or uncertain about their next steps. Instead of working on key tasks, they may find themselves browsing social media for hours. What may seem like a simple distraction often masks deeper issues: fear of failure, imposter syndrome, or a lack of clarity.

To effectively address the roots of distraction, consider these practical action steps:

I. Identify Personal Triggers: Observe and document the times when you're most tempted to veer off course. This helps you understand patterns and triggers that lead to distraction, like certain tasks or times of day.

II. Practice Intentional Technology Use: Set specific times to check messages and emails, turn off non-essential notifications, and create tech-free zones. This helps limit impulsive tech usage and enhances focus.

III. Establish Daily Priorities: Begin each day by listing your top goals and aligning tasks accordingly. This keeps your focus on core objectives and reduces susceptibility to distractions that don't align with your priorities.

IV. Manage Physical and Mental Clutter: A clutter-free workspace supports mental clarity. Similarly, addressing any lingering worries or unresolved decisions can help keep your mind focused.

V. Use Mindfulness Techniques: Take regular, short breaks to practice mindfulness. This enhances your ability to recognize distraction as it arises, enabling quicker refocus and reinforcing your awareness.

VI. Limit Multitasking: Focus on one task at a time. Multitasking divides attention and increases cognitive load, which can heighten susceptibility to distraction.

VII. Apply the Pomodoro Technique: Work in short, focused intervals (e.g., 25 minutes), followed by a brief break. This structure minimizes fatigue and helps maintain a consistent focus.

VIII. Reward Discipline, Not Distraction: Condition yourself to associate small rewards with completing focused work rather than indulging in distractions.

2. The Science Behind Procrastination

Procrastination is complex and stems from a range of psychological factors. One of the key explanations lies in our brain's wiring—specifically, the tension between the amygdala (responsible for immediate pleasure-seeking) and the prefrontal cortex (responsible for planning and self-control). When the amygdala wins, instant gratification becomes more appealing than delayed rewards, leading us to prioritize easier, enjoyable activities over essential but potentially challenging tasks.

Procrastination is a deeply ingrained habit rooted in psychological, neurological, and even evolutionary factors. It stems from the brain's tendency to prioritize short-term comfort over long-term gains, driven largely by the interplay between two key brain regions: the prefrontal cortex and the limbic system. Understanding these dynamics can help you rewire your response to avoid unnecessary delay.

3. Why We Procrastinate: Key Psychological Insights

I. The Instant Gratification Principle: Humans are naturally drawn to immediate rewards. The limbic system, responsible for emotions and survival instincts, favours activities that provide instant gratification (like checking social media) over those that delay reward (like finishing a complex project). When faced with a challenging task, your brain often defaults to activities that provide instant pleasure, diverting you from your longer-term goals.

II. Avoidance of Negative Emotions: Procrastination is frequently a response to negative emotions such as anxiety, self-doubt, or fear of failure. When a task seems overwhelming or likely to lead to discomfort, the brain may trigger avoidance as a coping mechanism, protecting you in the short term from the perceived pain but often worsening long-term stress as deadlines approach.

III. Lack of Clear Reward Pathways: Tasks that lack immediate rewards, such as projects with delayed benefits, create less motivation. Without visible progress markers, the brain struggles to stay engaged. Building smaller, intermediate rewards can help.

IV. Temporal Discounting: Temporal discounting is the tendency to value immediate rewards over future rewards. Neuroscientists believe this bias is partly evolutionary, as prioritizing immediate rewards helped early humans survive. However, it can lead to self-sabotage in a modern context, especially with tasks like saving for retirement or completing long-term goals, where the benefits feel far away.

V. The Role of Cognitive Dissonance: Cognitive dissonance—the mental discomfort of holding contradictory beliefs—can also play a role in procrastination. If you value achievement but find a task difficult or tedious, the brain seeks ways to minimize this discomfort, often by delaying the task altogether.

4. Action Steps to Combat Procrastination

I. Use **"Temptation Bundling":** Pair a less desirable task with something you enjoy. For instance, if you procrastinate on organizing your work files, listen to a favourite podcast while you do it. This technique leverages the limbic system's craving for immediate pleasure, helping you stay engaged in less enjoyable tasks.

II. **Practice Self-Compassion:** People who are hard on themselves for procrastinating often get stuck in a cycle of shame and avoidance. Research shows that treating yourself with kindness, and acknowledging your challenges without judgment, can break this cycle and foster a more productive mindset.

III. **Apply the "5-Minute Rule":** Commit to working on a task for just five minutes. Often, the hardest part of starting is overcoming the brain's resistance. Once you begin, it's easier to stay engaged. This approach helps your brain transition from a state of avoidance to one of productivity, leveraging momentum.

IV. **Visualize Future Rewards:** Use visualization to "see" yourself enjoying the rewards of completed tasks. Studies show that vividly imagining positive outcomes, like completing a report early or achieving career growth, can engage the brain's reward centres and reduce temporal discounting, making the long-term benefit feel more immediate.

V. **Break Tasks into Micro-Steps:** Large tasks often feel overwhelming, triggering avoidance. By dividing tasks into micro-steps, you activate the brain's dopamine pathways, which reward incremental progress and reduce the likelihood of feeling overwhelmed.

VI. **Limit Distractions with Physical Cues:** Environment plays a significant role in focus. Remove or reduce visual and auditory distractions, such as mobile phones or notifications, when you start a task. Physical reminders of focus, like a closed door or dedicated workspace, signal to the brain that it's time to work, creating conditions for engagement.

VII. **Reframe the Task's Value:** When a task feels meaningless, the brain resists it. Reframe the task by linking it to personal or career values. If you're writing a report, remind yourself that it builds your expertise, positioning you for future success. This approach helps the brain assign greater intrinsic value to the task.

VIII. **Reward Progress Regularly:** The brain responds well to positive reinforcement. Establish small rewards for completing each step of a task, like a short break or a small treat. This strategy helps build a pattern of achievement and engagement, ultimately reducing procrastination.

Procrastination is not a reflection of laziness but a complex interplay between your brain's reward system and emotional responses. By understanding the science behind why you procrastinate and applying practical techniques to redirect focus, you empower yourself to take control, reduce procrastination, and cultivate a disciplined approach to your goals. Over time, building habits like these enhances both productivity and self-confidence, reinforcing a mindset that values purpose over immediate comfort.

5. Strategies for Building a Distraction-Free Environment

While some distractions are inevitable, creating a conducive environment can significantly enhance focus and productivity. Here are a few practical steps:

I. *Designate a Dedicated Work Space:* Create a clear boundary between work and personal life by designating specific areas for specific activities. For example, working from home may become more productive by creating a designated workspace free of non-work items.

II. *Limit Digital Interruptions:* Notifications can derail even the most focused individuals. Tools like "Do Not Disturb" modes, email filters, and focus applications (like Forest or Freedom) can help block distractions and allow you to focus on high-priority tasks.

III. *Set Boundaries with Others:* Explain to colleagues, family, or friends that you're unavailable during specific times. By communicating these boundaries, you'll reduce interruptions and reinforce your commitment to focus.

IV. *Practice the "Two-Minute Rule" for Quick Tasks:* If a task takes less than two minutes, do it immediately rather than letting it pile up as a source of distraction. By quickly addressing minor tasks, you free up mental space for more important work.

6. Cultivating a Mindset of Self-Discipline

Building and maintaining a distraction-free lifestyle also relies heavily on mental discipline. Here are some powerful mindset shifts to help:

I. *Accept Imperfection:* Perfectionism is often a hidden form of procrastination. Instead of aiming for flawless results, aim for steady progress. Realize that improvement is more important than perfection.

II. *Embrace Delayed Gratification:* Training yourself to delay gratification can reduce impulsive decisions. Try experimenting with small exercises like delaying dessert until you've completed a set task, building up the habit of choosing long-term rewards over immediate pleasure.

III. *Focus on Purpose and Vision:* Remind yourself why you're pursuing your goals and the long-term benefits of staying disciplined. Writing down your vision and purpose helps you stay aligned with meaningful goals rather than being swayed by temporary distractions.

7. Real-World Examples of Overcoming Distractions and Procrastination

Deep Work at Infosys: In the competitive tech industry, Infosys, one of India's leading IT firms, emphasizes creating a "deep work" culture. To foster focus, Infosys has introduced dedicated deep-work zones where employees can work without interruptions. This culture encourages employees to block time for high-focus activities, reducing digital distractions and promoting productivity.

Apple and Prioritization: Globally, Apple's culture is an example of disciplined prioritization. Steve Jobs famously cut down Apple's product line from dozens of models to just a few core offerings, allowing the company to focus and perfect each product. This ruthless prioritization wasn't only a company strategy but also a testament to Jobs' philosophy of minimizing distractions to concentrate on what matters most.

8. Managing Procrastination with Time Management Techniques

Time management techniques can be a crucial asset in fighting procrastination. Methods like Time Blocking and the Pomodoro Technique encourage structured work habits:

I. *Time Blocking:* Schedule dedicated blocks of time for each task and stick to it. This technique helps in visualizing time and brings structure to the day. Leaders like Elon Musk use this method to ensure they stay productive across multiple responsibilities.

II. *The Pomodoro Technique:* Work for 25 minutes followed by a 5-minute break, repeating this cycle four times before taking a longer break. This approach keeps your brain refreshed and helps maintain focus over extended periods without mental exhaustion.

9. Building Accountability for Better Results

I. *Accountability Partners:* One effective way to overcome procrastination is to create accountability with a trusted friend or colleague. When you know someone else is aware of your goals, it can motivate you to stay committed and avoid excuses. An accountability partner can be anyone—a friend, a mentor, or a peer who is also working towards their goals.

II. *Public Accountability:* Public accountability can be powerful for personal transformation. For example, using social media to share your goals with friends or followers creates a sense of commitment. Public declarations make it harder to back out without risking embarrassment or letting down your audience.

III. *Self-Tracking Tools and Metrics:* Using productivity apps like Trello, Notion, or even a simple journal helps track daily tasks and progress, creating a sense of achievement when checking items off. Tracking tools bring awareness to patterns of procrastination and enable adjustments for improved focus and productivity.

10. The Power of Choice

Overcoming distractions and procrastination is not about reaching a state of perfection but about choosing to take action each day, regardless of setbacks. Each choice to refocus on your goals and each small victory over procrastination builds the habit of discipline. Learning to confront distractions and manage procrastination is not just an exercise in productivity—it is a declaration of commitment to personal growth and excellence.

This discipline-driven approach to tackling the modern-day challenges of distraction and procrastination empowers individuals to not only achieve their ambitions but to live purposefully, driving continuous improvement in every area of life. The journey may not be easy, but the rewards—personal satisfaction, professional success, and the respect that comes from self-mastery—are well worth the effort.

Overcoming distractions and procrastination is essential for achieving personal and professional goals. It begins with recognizing the patterns and triggers that lead to procrastination and distractions and implementing practical strategies like time blocking, prioritization, and mindfulness. Building self-discipline, creating an environment conducive to focus, and breaking tasks into manageable steps can significantly enhance productivity. Embracing progress over perfection helps maintain momentum and reduces the fear of starting. Regular self-reflection and adjusting strategies ensure continued improvement in managing time and focus. With consistent effort and intentional habits, overcoming these obstacles becomes a stepping stone to sustained success.

Purpose doesn't just give life meaning; it gives every day a direction

Chapter 7

Accountability and Social Support

Accountability and social support are vital but often underappreciated pillars of success. Many aspiring leaders, entrepreneurs, and professionals might assume they can *"do it alone"* with sheer willpower. However, research and real-world experiences repeatedly show that individuals who build strong networks of accountability partners and cultivate social support are far more likely to stick to their goals, achieve sustainable success, and navigate challenges effectively. While self-motivation drives initial progress, sustainable growth often requires external reinforcement; whether through a mentor, peer group, or support network that champions your ambitions and holds you responsible for your commitments.

Studies on successful leaders and entrepreneurs reveal how many of them attribute a part of their success to the accountability mechanisms they put in place. In India, entrepreneurs like Falguni Nayar, founder of Nykaa, and globally, leaders like Satya Nadella of Microsoft demonstrate how engaging with trusted mentors and advisors has strengthened their disciplined pursuit of business goals.

Whether through accountability partnerships, formal coaching, or group-based systems, harnessing social support not only complements personal discipline but often transforms the journey, making it more rewarding and less isolating.

1. Accountability as a Catalyst for Discipline

Accountability acts as a bridge between intention and action. When we publicly declare our goals to others, we create a psychological contract that motivates us to stay disciplined and follow through. This principle holds true across various sectors and professions. In India's IT industry, Infosys has cultivated a culture of accountability by promoting openness and regular feedback mechanisms among team members, empowering individuals to remain aligned with the company's objectives and personal goals alike.

Accountability helps us internalize our commitments. In many ways, it becomes a feedback loop where each action (or inaction) is observed, evaluated, and adjusted. Even personal goals like exercise, diet, or reading habits can be positively reinforced through accountability measures, such as logging daily progress or sharing updates with a friend or coach.

2. Practical Strategies for Creating Accountability

Accountability is the cornerstone of personal and professional success. It ensures that commitments are honoured, goals are achieved, and growth remains consistent. Whether it's staying true to individual objectives or aligning team efforts in a workplace, accountability fosters trust, discipline, and results. However, accountability is not automatic, it requires intentional strategies to set clear expectations, track progress, and encourage responsibility.

Let us explore some actionable techniques to help create accountability. These strategies are designed to help individuals and teams stay on course, take ownership of their actions, and deliver on their promises.

I. Identify a Trusted Accountability Partner: This individual could be a friend, mentor, colleague, or coach—someone who can offer honest feedback and encouragement. Silicon Valley's entrepreneurial ecosystem encourages "accountability buddies," where founders frequently check in with one another to track progress and offer support.

II. *Set Clear, Measurable Goals Together*: Defining specific milestones with your accountability partner is key to making this partnership effective. When the goals are vague, accountability loses its grounding. Implement goal-setting frameworks that emphasize transparency and specificity, allowing you both to keep each other accountable.

III. *Regular Check-ins and Reviews*: Consistent check-ins help keep momentum going. These could be daily, weekly, or even monthly meetings depending on the nature of the goal. An executive coach for instance often includes regular progress updates, helping high-level leaders stay accountable to their professional and personal objectives. Entrepreneurs can schedule bi-weekly calls with their accountability partners to discuss their progress and potential obstacles.

IV. *Embrace Constructive Feedback:* Receiving feedback can be challenging, especially if it highlights our shortcomings. However, an effective accountability partner offers constructive criticism in a way that promotes growth. Ray Dalio, founder of Bridgewater Associates, fosters a radically transparent culture in his company. This openness to feedback, even when it is hard to hear, has been instrumental in building discipline and resilience within the organization.

3. The Role of Social Support in Sustaining Discipline

Social support can come from various sources: friends, family, colleagues, mentors, or professional groups. It provides the emotional and practical resources to help us remain resilient in the face of obstacles. From a psychological perspective, social support reduces stress and boosts mental well-being, which can be crucial when pursuing long-term goals that require a high level of discipline.

Zoho Corporation Founder Sridhar Vembu's approach to team-building goes beyond the professional sphere, as he has relocated a significant portion of the company's operations to rural areas, fostering a culture of community support and well-being. By embedding social support into the workplace, Zoho has enhanced employee morale and productivity, ultimately leading to greater individual and organizational discipline.

Priya, is an amateur runner in Mumbai aiming to complete her first marathon. While her goal was deeply personal, Priya knew she would need structure and support to stick to her demanding schedule. She joined a local running club, where fellow members held her accountable to weekly long runs and provided encouragement during difficult phases. On days when her motivation waned, the commitment to her group pulled her through, reminding her of her progress and long-term goal. The collective accountability helped Priya not only achieve physical fitness but also taught her resilience and mental discipline—qualities that extended to her personal and professional life. Her running group provided motivation, encouragement, and a shared sense of purpose, illustrating how social support can reinforce personal discipline and endurance, helping individuals push through challenges and achieve their ambitions.

4. Practical Ways to Build Social Support

Building meaningful social support networks requires effort and intentionality. It's not just about having a large circle of acquaintances but cultivating relationships based on trust, mutual respect, and shared values. Let us explore some practical strategies for nurturing supportive relationships, leveraging community resources, and creating environments that encourage collaboration and empathy. These approaches can strengthen your personal and professional network, helping you thrive in all areas of life.

I. *Join or Form Mastermind Groups*: Mastermind groups are gatherings of like-minded individuals who meet regularly to share insights, support each other's goals, and hold one another accountable. Companies like Google and Facebook encourage mastermind-like discussions within their teams to spark innovation, solve problems collaboratively, and provide social support for challenging projects. By connecting with a group that shares your values and aspirations, you create a network that propels you forward.

II. *Engage with Mentorship Programs:* Mentorship is one of the most impactful forms of social support. Finding a mentor who has walked the path you're on can provide you with valuable guidance and moral support. Initiatives like the "Mentor India" program enable young entrepreneurs to gain insights from industry veterans, helping them navigate early challenges and stay focused on their goals.

III. *Cultivate Supportive Personal Relationships*: Our personal relationships can be powerful sources of encouragement. Sharing your goals with family members or close friends and asking for their support can be instrumental in staying disciplined. Sundar Pichai, CEO of Google, has openly credited his family's support as a crucial factor in his journey. Recognizing and nurturing these bonds can add resilience to our personal discipline.

IV. *Engage in Community-Based Initiatives*: Being part of a community initiative fosters a sense of belonging and purpose. Many professionals find that engaging in volunteer work or social projects reinvigorates their drive and reminds them of the larger purpose behind their goals. Companies like Wipro in India actively encourage employees to participate in social responsibility projects, which has led to greater employee engagement and personal accountability.

5. Balancing Accountability with Self-Compassion

Balancing accountability with self-compassion is a crucial skill for fostering both resilience and sustainable growth. While accountability pushes individuals to hold themselves to high standards, self-compassion provides a supportive counterbalance, allowing for forgiveness and encouragement in moments of failure or struggle. Together, they prevent burnout and promote steady progress, helping individuals avoid the pitfalls of harsh self-criticism.

When striving to meet challenging goals, accountability encourages consistent effort and adherence to set plans, often leveraging support from others, like mentors or accountability partners. However, setbacks are inevitable, and a purely accountability-driven mindset can result in self-criticism, guilt, or even discouragement, if goals aren't consistently met. Here, self-compassion offers a healthy perspective, reminding individuals to approach mistakes as learning opportunities and recognize the hard work invested so far.

By blending both approaches, individuals create a sustainable model of discipline where they are motivated to persist without fearing failure. They learn to course-correct with patience, viewing each setback as a moment to refine strategies and adjust their pace. This balance strengthens mental resilience, creating a discipline that is driven not only by external milestones but also by a kind and constructive inner dialogue.

Jeff Weiner, the former CEO of LinkedIn was known for his focus on compassionate leadership, emphasizing the importance of empathy in the workplace. When LinkedIn faced challenges, such as missed financial targets, Weiner held himself accountable by addressing these issues head-on with transparency and responsibility. At the same time, he encouraged his team to practice self-compassion, reminding them that setbacks were part of the growth process and that they should learn from them without being overly critical of themselves.

This balance helped create a resilient culture at LinkedIn, where employees were not only driven by high standards but also felt supported during tough times. Instead of pushing people to meet goals at all costs, Weiner fostered an environment where accountability coexisted with understanding and personal growth, reinforcing the idea that growth requires both pushing oneself and being kind to oneself in the face of adversity.

Embracing setbacks as part of the journey can help aspiring leaders and entrepreneurs maintain their focus without falling into self-doubt or over-criticism.

In a world that prizes independence, accountability, and social support offer a refreshing contrast. They underscore the fact that discipline is not only a personal endeavour but also a shared commitment. As aspiring leaders, entrepreneurs, and professionals work towards their personal and career goals, harnessing accountability and support networks can significantly boost their likelihood of success.

These networks not only create a sense of shared responsibility but also provide a safety net during difficult times. Whether it's a regular check-in with an accountability buddy or participation in a mastermind group, these measures collectively cultivate a disciplined life anchored by purpose and community. As the demands of modern life continue to rise, the importance of accountability and social support remains a timeless strategy for anyone on the journey to personal excellence.

When motivation fades, discipline keeps the fire burning

Chapter 8

Mindfulness

Mindfulness, the practice of being fully present in the moment without judgment, has rapidly gained recognition as a transformative tool for personal growth and discipline. It's often seen as a practice for enhancing well-being, reducing stress, and improving focus. But what many may not realize is that mindfulness is also a critical component in achieving sustained discipline, especially for those of us striving for excellence in our personal and professional lives.

In today's world, where distractions are aplenty and the pressure to perform is constant, mindfulness becomes not just an optional tool, but a necessary practice to build the focus and mental toughness required for disciplined living. Discipline is often seen as sheer willpower, but mindfulness reframes it as a conscious choice - an alignment of intentions with deliberate actions. Whether you're an aspiring leader looking to improve your leadership capabilities, an entrepreneur trying to scale your business, or an ambitious professional trying to achieve your career goals, mindfulness is a bridge that can link you directly to a life of disciplined purpose.

Let's start by understanding why mindfulness is so powerful in nurturing discipline. Mindfulness brings clarity to your thoughts and emotions, creating space between your impulses and actions. This space is crucial because it allows you to make conscious, intentional decisions rather than reacting impulsively to every distraction, challenge, or emotional trigger that comes your way. This is where discipline begins: in the moment of choice - when you decide to either give in to the urge or stay true to your purpose.

By practicing and integrating mindfulness into daily life, you can develop greater self-control, improve emotional regulation, and reduce the mental clutter that often leads to procrastination or impulsive behaviour. Whether through meditation, mindful breathing, or simply paying full attention to tasks at hand, mindfulness equips us to respond thoughtfully rather than react instinctively. By embracing mindfulness, you can create a foundation of calm focus that empowers sustained growth and achievement in all areas of life.

1. The Neuroscience Behind Mindfulness and Discipline

Mindfulness has a profound effect on the brain. Research has shown that it activates regions of the brain responsible for self-regulation, focus, and decision-making. It enhances the prefrontal cortex—the brain's command centre, responsible for executive functions like planning, judgment, and impulse control—while simultaneously quieting the amygdala, the part of the brain that processes emotions and can trigger knee-jerk reactions.

The hippocampus, vital for memory and emotional regulation, also benefits with mindfulness, increasing its gray matter density and reducing the harmful effects of chronic stress. These changes contribute to better emotional resilience and cognitive performance. This biological shift helps individuals remain calm, focused, and disciplined even in high-pressure situations, ultimately enhancing their capacity for sustained focus and disciplined action in pursuit of goals.

For instance, when faced with a stressful situation at work, a mindful individual is able to pause and consider their response, rather than allowing anxiety or frustration to take control. The decision to act with composure and rationality in high-pressure moments is precisely the kind of discipline that leads to long-term success. On the other hand, individuals who allow their emotions to drive them may succumb to distractions or make rash decisions that undermine their goals. The ability to pause and reflect, cultivated through mindfulness, is what allows a disciplined individual to remain focused on their long-term objectives.

2. Real-World Example: The Power of Mindfulness in Business

Take the example of the late Ratan Tata, the former chairman of the Tata Group, one of India's largest and most respected conglomerates. His leadership was built not just on strategic thinking, but on a deep sense of mindfulness in his decision-making process. Tata was known for his calm, composed demeanour in the face of adversity, whether it was during the financial crisis of 2008 or when the group acquired global companies like Jaguar Land Rover. He often emphasized the importance of listening—not just to others but also to oneself. "There's always a need to reflect, to take a moment before making a decision," Tata once said. This moment of reflection—this practice of mindfulness - allowed him to maintain discipline in his decisions and helped him steer the vast empire with purpose and focus.

Tata's approach highlights how mindfulness can give leaders the clarity and emotional control they need to make balanced decisions in high-stakes situations, a hallmark of disciplined leadership.

Another powerful example of mindfulness in business comes from Aetna, a U.S.-based health insurance company.

In 2010, CEO Mark Bertolini introduced a mindfulness program for employees to help reduce stress and improve overall well-being. The program, which included meditation and yoga, led to noticeable improvements in productivity, engagement, and a reduction in healthcare costs for the company. Aetna reported a 28% reduction in stress levels, along with a 20% increase in productivity. This demonstrated that mindful practices could drive both personal well-being and organizational performance.

Yet another notable example of the power of mindfulness at an individual level in business comes from Arianna Huffington, the founder of The Huffington Post and now CEO of Thrive Global. After experiencing burnout that led to a serious health crisis, she began practicing mindfulness and meditation daily. This shift not only improved her health but also helped her become more focused, present, and empathetic in her leadership role. Her personal transformation has influenced the broader corporate culture at Thrive Global, which now advocates for mindfulness practices to improve workplace productivity and mental well-being.

3. Mindfulness and Self-Control: Cultivating the Habit of Consistent Action

The essence of mindfulness is being aware of your thoughts, emotions, and bodily sensations without judgment. This awareness allows you to detach from automatic responses and develop a deeper understanding of why you do the things you do. When you bring this awareness to your habits and routines, it becomes much easier to identify areas where you may be lacking discipline and take proactive steps to improve.

Imagine an entrepreneur working tirelessly to grow a startup. The challenges are endless, and the temptation to give in to distractions or procrastinate is constant. But when you cultivate mindfulness, you become more aware of your tendencies. You notice when you're drifting off course, and you have the mental clarity to bring yourself back to what matters most. Instead of mindlessly scrolling through social media or spending hours on tasks that don't contribute to your end goals, mindfulness helps you catch yourself in the act and redirect your focus back on the work that will drive your business forward.

Another inspiring example of a leader leveraging mindfulness is Marc Benioff, the CEO of Salesforce. He credits mindfulness practices, such as meditation and periods of reflective silence, with helping him maintain focus, clarity, and resilience during high-pressure situations. During times of crisis, Benioff uses mindfulness to stay grounded, make thoughtful decisions, and remain attuned to the needs of his team and stakeholders. By incorporating mindfulness into his leadership style, he has not only navigated challenges effectively but also fostered a company culture that values emotional intelligence and purpose-driven leadership.

4. The Daily Practice: How to Incorporate Mindfulness into Your Routine

Incorporating mindfulness into your daily routine does not require hours of practice or a complete overhaul of your lifestyle. In fact, it's the small, consistent moments of mindfulness, build over time, and create lasting change. Here are some practical strategies to integrate mindfulness into your daily life:

I. *Start Your Day with Intention:* The way you begin your day sets the tone for everything that follows. Begin each morning with a brief mindfulness practice. This could be as simple as spending five minutes focusing on your breath, setting your intentions for the day, or practicing gratitude. This helps centre your mind and prepares you to face the challenges of the day with purpose and clarity.

   A simple mindfulness practice could involve closing your eyes for a few minutes, breathing deeply, and reflecting on one or two key goals you want to focus on that day. By cantering your mind, you create a mental framework that promotes disciplined focus throughout your workday.

II. *Mindful Breaks*: Pause and Reset: It's easy to get caught up in the whirlwind of tasks and responsibilities, especially in high-pressure environments. However, constant hustle can lead to burnout and reduced productivity. Instead, take mindful breaks throughout your day to reset your energy and focus. This can be a few minutes of deep breathing, a short walk, or simply stepping away from your workspace to clear your mind.

This practice not only improves your mental clarity but also increases productivity. When you return to your work after a mindful break, you're better able to focus, think critically, and make disciplined decisions.

III. Practice Single-Tasking: In a world that encourages multitasking, mindfulness teaches the opposite: single-tasking. Focus on one task at a time, and bring your full attention to it. This requires discipline, but the rewards are immense. When you give your undivided attention to a task, you complete it with greater efficiency and precision.

IV. *Reflection*: End Your Day with Clarity: End your day by reflecting on your actions and decisions. What went well? What could have been done differently? This practice of self-reflection, combined with mindfulness, helps you learn from your experiences and improve your discipline moving forward. By reflecting on your day, you create the space to understand your successes and your setbacks, which are crucial for continued growth.

5. The Discipline of Mindfulness

Mindfulness is not just about being present in the moment; it's about using that presence to sharpen your discipline, achieve your goals, and live with intention. In the fast-paced, ever-changing world we live in, mindfulness offers a way to anchor ourselves to what truly matters. It provides us with the mental clarity to make disciplined decisions, the emotional resilience to handle challenges, and the self-awareness to stay aligned with our purpose.

By integrating mindfulness into your daily routine, you can unlock a new level of focus and discipline that will help you achieve your goals with greater ease. Like any practice, mindfulness requires consistency and commitment, but the rewards—improved focus, greater emotional control, and sustainable discipline—are well worth the effort.

As we've seen in the examples, mindfulness is not just a personal tool for well-being; it's a powerful leadership asset. It's one of the most effective ways to cultivate the discipline necessary for long-term success, both personally and professionally.

Discipline, when coupled with mindfulness, becomes a way of life—one that's intentional, purposeful, and aligned with your highest goals.

Practicing mindfulness:

- ***Set aside time***: *To start mindfulness, it's crucial to set aside a dedicated time each day. It can be as short as 10 minutes, but consistency is key. You can gradually increase the duration once you feel comfortable. Find a quiet space where you won't be disturbed, such as a corner in your home, a park bench, or even during your commute.*
- ***Focus on your breath***: *Start by observing your breath naturally. Feel the air coming in through your nostrils and expanding your chest or belly. If your mind starts to wander, gently guide your attention back to your breath. You may notice distractions like thoughts, emotions, or external noises, but acknowledge them without judgment and return to the sensation of breathing. Over time, this will build your ability to stay focused.*
- ***Body scan***: *The body scan technique involves mentally scanning your body from head to toe. Start with your toes, noticing any sensations—whether tension, relaxation, or temperature. Slowly move up to your feet, legs, abdomen, chest, and so on, paying attention to each part without rushing. This practice enhances body awareness and helps release any areas of tension, making it an effective method for relaxation.*

- ***Non-judgmental awareness:*** *As you practice mindfulness, you'll inevitably encounter thoughts or emotions that may distract you. Instead of fighting them or labelling them as good or bad, observe them with curiosity. Acknowledge their presence and then gently return your focus to your breath or body. This step fosters a sense of detachment from your emotions and thoughts, allowing them to pass without becoming overwhelmed by them.*
- ***Daily integration****: Mindfulness doesn't have to be confined to a set practice time. You can integrate it into your daily activities. Whether you're eating, walking, working, or having a conversation, you can practice mindfulness by focusing entirely on the present moment. For instance, when eating, notice the taste, texture, and smell of each bite. When walking, pay attention to how your body moves with each step. This approach trains your mind to stay present, reducing stress and increasing focus in everyday life.*

Find your purpose, and even the ordinary becomes extraordinary

Chapter 9

Transitions and Life Changes

Life transitions, whether personal or professional, are powerful forces that push us out of our comfort zones and challenge us to grow. These changes—such as career shifts, relocations, or personal milestones—test our resilience and reveal the strength of our discipline and adaptability. Each transition, while disruptive, holds the potential for profound personal growth when approached with structure, intention, and an open mind. Navigating these changes with purpose and resilience can be the difference between flourishing and merely surviving. By cultivating a disciplined approach to change, you can face life's inevitable transitions with confidence and clarity, transforming these phases into opportunities for growth and purpose.

We will delve into the art of navigating life's turning points with clarity and purpose, exploring how to anchor oneself amid change. Drawing lessons from individuals who've used discipline as a guiding principle during transformative phases, we will uncover strategies to stay focused, emotionally balanced, and goal-oriented. By breaking down change into manageable actions, we can transform life's uncertainties into a path of self-discovery and purpose-driven progress.

The aim here is to create a blueprint for handling transitions with grace and strength, ultimately transforming these phases into opportunities that align with our deepest values and aspirations. From setting micro-goals to managing emotions and creating supportive networks, this chapter provides the tools to approach change not as an obstacle but as a powerful gateway to a more purpose-driven life.

1. Embracing Change as a Catalyst for Growth

Embracing change is an essential mindset for anyone striving for personal or professional growth. While change often disrupts our routines, causing stress and discomfort, it also opens up opportunities for transformation that would otherwise remain untapped. Leaders, entrepreneurs, and individuals in pursuit of self-improvement often find that leaning into change, rather than resisting it, helps them grow beyond what they thought possible.

First, it's important to view change as a constructive force. Often, change brings hidden benefits, revealing new aspects of our abilities, interests, or limitations. For instance, when leaders face major shifts, they are forced to reassess their skills and strengthen areas that may have previously been overlooked. This process of re-evaluation sharpens both character and purpose, fostering resilience and insight. Those who consciously approach change as a means of self-improvement are more likely to emerge stronger and more skilled.

Consider the experience of a seasoned professional who transitions into a different industry after years of familiarity. At first, the learning curve can be overwhelming, requiring adaptation to new technologies, company cultures, or market demands. However, by embracing this transition with a growth-oriented mindset, they can acquire fresh perspectives and skills. Similarly, whether you're changing jobs, starting a business, or moving to a new city, it's crucial to maintain a mindset that views change as an opportunity to grow. A disciplined approach to managing transitions requires setting clear intentions and cultivating resilience through both strategic planning and self-awareness.

Another critical factor in using change for growth is the importance of self-discipline. During transitions, structured discipline provides stability amid chaos, offering a sense of control and continuity. For example, setting micro-goals allows individuals to track incremental progress, thereby building momentum. This focus on short-term objectives prevents the sense of overwhelm that often accompanies major life shifts, giving the individual a clear direction. Embracing structured practices, like daily reflection or goal-setting, ensures that each step forward aligns with larger objectives, no matter how disruptive the change.

Moreover, change becomes a catalyst for growth when we actively seek learning opportunities within it. This involves cultivating a mindset that sees every challenge as a lesson and every setback as a chance to learn. A disciplined approach to self-assessment, such as journaling or regular feedback loops, allows individuals to recognize patterns, make adjustments, and grow in response to feedback. Leaders who embrace change not only improve personally but also inspire those around them by demonstrating resilience and adaptability.

Embracing change as a growth catalyst is about transforming uncertainty into opportunity. Through disciplined practices, a willingness to learn, and an attitude that welcomes challenge, you can unlock new levels of self-awareness, resilience, and achievement. By viewing change not as an obstacle but as a powerful motivator, we open ourselves up to a future rich with potential and purpose.

2. Developing Self-Discipline Amid Uncertainty

One of the greatest challenges of navigating transitions is the uncertainty that accompanies change. Our instincts often resist uncertainty, but disciplined individuals learn to embrace it. Developing self-discipline involves practicing small, purposeful habits that help you stay centred and focused, regardless of external chaos.

In times of uncertainty, self-discipline becomes one of the most reliable tools to navigate challenges effectively. It acts as a stabilizing force, providing consistency and control when external circumstances seem unpredictable. By establishing structured routines, setting short-term achievable goals, and committing to personal standards, self-discipline can help you maintain focus, reduce stress, and work steadily toward long-term objectives, even when the environment is volatile.

A way to nurture self-discipline is to establish non-negotiable habits that promote well-being and mental clarity. Even a simple, structured morning routine—such as meditation, exercise, or journaling—can ground you, instilling a sense of calm before the day's unpredictability unfolds. Many high-performing professionals adopt mindfulness practices to maintain focus and emotional stability, helping them to respond to changes rather than react impulsively.

Uncertainty often brings heightened stress with it, making resilience a necessary counterpart to discipline. Building resilience involves a disciplined approach to mental conditioning, such as reframing challenges as opportunities for growth, maintaining a positive mindset, and using setbacks as learning experiences. Think of it as a practice of mental endurance: the ability to keep moving forward despite setbacks by remaining focused on values and long-term goals.

Developing self-discipline in uncertain times calls for a commitment to continuous learning and flexibility. By embracing a growth mindset, you can stay adaptable and open to change, using new insights to adjust your strategies as situations evolve. This involves setting aside time for self-reflection and continuous improvement, allowing you to fine-tune your approach based on real-world feedback. Leaders like Sheryl Sandberg during her transition from Google to Facebook is an apt example. Entering Facebook at a critical time in the company's history, she implemented disciplined strategies to improve its advertising model. She faced a rapidly changing environment but managed to stay consistent and goal-focused, channelling her discipline to steer Facebook's monetization efforts with remarkable success. By committing to consistency in her strategies, Sandberg exemplified how disciplined habits can anchor you during periods of flux.

In your own transitions, adopting similar methods can ground you. Daily practices, such as setting micro-goals serve as points of stability, anchoring you even as other aspects of life evolve. While we can't control external factors, self-discipline enables us to manage our internal responses, making it possible to navigate uncertainty with purpose and steady progress toward meaningful goals.

3. Setting Goals and Micro-Goals for Transition Periods

Transition periods, whether they involve a career shift, personal growth, or life change, can feel overwhelming due to the sheer volume of adjustments needed. Setting clear goals and micro-goals during these times can create a structured path forward, breaking the journey into manageable steps that build momentum and confidence along the way. This approach fosters a sense of control, ensuring that progress remains visible even in times of flux, while also allowing flexibility to adapt to unforeseen circumstances.

A practical first step in goal-setting during transitions is to establish a clear vision of what success looks like post-transition. This "big picture" goal might include long-term career aspirations, personal life objectives, or desired lifestyle changes. This broader vision serves as the foundation, reminding you of your ultimate purpose and helping to realign efforts when distractions or setbacks occur. For instance, someone transitioning to a leadership role may define success as building a cohesive, high-performing team within the first year. This vision provides direction, anchoring decisions and actions.

Once a big-picture goal is defined, breaking it down into actionable micro-goals becomes essential. Micro-goals are specific, short-term objectives that guide immediate actions and provide a sense of accomplishment. For instance, in the case of the aspiring leader, initial micro-goals might include completing a leadership training program, scheduling regular one-on-one meetings with team members, or identifying mentors within the company. Each of these steps directly supports the larger goal of team cohesion by building essential skills, relationships, and knowledge.

This approach is effective because each micro-goal acts as a marker of progress. Psychologically, the brain responds positively to incremental achievements. According to behavioural psychology, the dopamine released with each small victory reinforces the motivation to keep moving forward, building confidence as you complete each step.

Transitions often cloud one's sense of purpose, making clear and precise goal-setting crucial. SMART goals—specific, measurable, achievable, relevant, and time-bound—become especially valuable. For instance, instead of aiming broadly to "adapt to change," make it measurable by setting a goal like, "From Monday, 1st Dec, at - PM / - AM establish a daily routine that includes 15 minutes of **personal reflection***". Clarity provides direction and reduces the chances of feeling lost during transitions. Setting SMART goals forces you to define success in practical terms, ensuring that each goal contributes to your overarching objectives and reflects your evolving priorities.

Guide to Practice Personal Reflection:

Personal reflection is a deliberate process of looking inward to analyse thoughts, feelings, and actions, fostering personal growth and clarity. Here is how you can practice it:

- ***Set Aside Time and Space**: Choose a quiet, distraction-free environment where you can focus. Dedicate consistent time, such as mornings or evenings, to build a habit.*
- ***Identify a Focus Area**: Reflect on specific themes like recent experiences, personal goals, relationships, or challenges*
- ***Use a Medium for Reflection**: Write in a journal to articulate thoughts. You could also record audio reflections and meditate silently to process feelings.*
- ***Ask Open-Ended Questions**: What did I learn today? Why did I react the way I did? What can I improve moving forward? Dive deep into "why" behind your actions to uncover patterns and motivations.*

- ***Incorporate Gratitude**: Reflect on positive moments and what you're thankful for. This shifts focus to solutions and strengths.*
- ***Review and Act**: Periodically revisit your reflections to identify recurring themes or progress. Create actionable steps to address insights gained during reflection.*

Micro-goals are uniquely positioned to help maintain momentum, especially when larger goals feel distant or challenging. By creating goals that can be achieved within a week or even a day, you can generate a steady rhythm of accomplishment. For example, if adapting to a new city, your first micro-goal might be as simple as "explore one new neighbourhood this weekend." Each small step feeds into the larger goal, helping you integrate into the environment gradually.

I. Develop Short-Term and Long-Term Goal Layers: Transitions often involve both short-term adjustments and long-term growth, so a layered approach to goal-setting can help address both. For instance, if you're starting a new business, short-term goals might include "setting up a professional network within three months," while long-term goals could include "achieving profitability within two years." Layering these goals ensures that both immediate and future needs are met, providing stability now while building toward lasting success.

To manage these layers, consider using visual goal-mapping techniques, like mind maps or digital project management tools, which help you visualize short-term steps within the context of larger aspirations. Layered goals ensure you can maintain focus on immediate needs without losing sight of the broader vision.

II. Regularly Reassess Goals to Stay Aligned: Transitions can bring unexpected changes, so it's essential to regularly assess and adjust your goals to ensure they remain relevant. Schedule monthly or quarterly reviews where you evaluate your progress, celebrate achievements, and recalibrate if needed. For instance, if a particular micro-goal, like mastering a new skill, turns out to be too challenging within the expected timeline, adjust it to something more feasible or extend the timeline. Flexibility keeps goals relevant, meaningful, and motivating, even as circumstances shift.

III. Embrace Each Micro-Goal as a Learning Opportunity: Finally, treat each micro-goal as a chance to learn and grow, rather than solely as a task to be completed. Transitions are inherently times of learning, and each step forward brings new insights. For instance, if a goal is to give a presentation in a new job, focus on your subject knowledge, what you learned about public speaking, audience engagement, or your own strengths as a presenter. Reflecting on these learnings after each goal completion can deepen self-awareness and adaptability, essential qualities for navigating transitions successfully.

Another key benefit of micro-goals during transition periods is their ability to counteract inertia or self-doubt, common challenges in uncertain times. By focusing on small achievements, you can experience regular progress, which reinforces motivation and builds resilience. For example, during a career change, micro-goals might include researching new industries, attending networking events, connecting with your ex-colleagues and managers, or applying to a certain number of jobs per week. Each of these small actions contributes to a larger career shift, making the transition feel attainable through consistent, measurable progress.

When Deepinder Goyal founded Zomato, he was stepping into a new realm of online food delivery in India, a concept that was nascent at the time. By setting short-term, achievable goals, he built Zomato step by step, eventually leading it to become a major player in the global food-tech space. His disciplined approach to incremental progress allowed him to pivot and adapt to market demands without losing sight of his overall purpose.

Setting and achieving goals and micro-goals during transitions involves clarity, structure, and adaptability. By dividing larger objectives into smaller, actionable steps, you maintain momentum, foster resilience, and create a sense of accomplishment. This framework for goal-setting not only facilitates a smoother transition but also strengthens your self-discipline, setting a foundation for growth and success in all areas of life.

4. Managing Emotional Resilience Through Change

Transitions often trigger an array of emotions: anxiety, fear, excitement, and even doubt. Managing these emotions requires self-discipline, particularly in developing a mindful and emotionally intelligent response to challenges. Emotional resilience can be fortified through intentional practices such as mindfulness, self-reflection, and constructive self-talk.

Indra Nooyi, former CEO of PepsiCo, frequently highlighted the importance of emotional intelligence and resilience in her journey. As an immigrant navigating corporate America and leading a Fortune 500 company, she faced numerous personal and professional transitions. Nooyi maintained her focus and composure by grounding herself in her values, a practice that strengthened her resilience in moments of change.

Strengthening this resilience involves several key practices. These practices help you process emotions constructively and maintain mental clarity. Remember that resilience isn't about avoiding challenges but rather approaching them with a mindset that is both flexible and disciplined.

I. **Acceptance of Change:** Rather than resisting change, practice acceptance by acknowledging that change is a constant part of life. Shifting from resistance to openness helps ease the emotional strain of transitions. For example, rather than focusing on the comfort of an old job or routine, try reframing the new situation as an opportunity for growth. This mental shift can reduce stress and foster a more positive outlook.

II. **Building Emotional Awareness:** Recognize and label emotions as they arise. This helps in managing them constructively rather than being overwhelmed. Practicing mindfulness can assist with this process, allowing you to identify emotions without judgment. When you're feeling anxious or uncertain, for example, try to pause and reflect on the underlying causes of these emotions, which helps in addressing them rather than reacting impulsively.

III. **Using Positive Self-Talk:** Language shapes perception, and self-talk can significantly influence resilience. Reframe negative thoughts with constructive self-dialogue. Instead of thinking, "I can't handle this," try, "I can take it one step at a time." This type of language reinforces confidence and reinforces mental toughness during challenging times.

IV. **Setting Emotional Boundaries:** During periods of change, it's crucial to set boundaries to protect your emotional energy. Declining unnecessary commitments or minimizing exposure to stressful environments can preserve your focus and resilience. For example, limit time spent around negative influences or take breaks from news cycles if they are causing additional stress.

V. **Seeking Support Networks:** Connect with others for support, whether through friends, family, or mentors. Support networks provide perspective, encouragement, and guidance, reminding you that you're not alone in navigating change. Openly sharing your challenges with a trusted network can alleviate emotional burdens, offering both relief and insights on how others might have managed similar situations.

VI. **Prioritizing Self-Care Routines:** Physical well-being influences emotional resilience. Consistent sleep, a balanced diet, and regular exercise directly impact mental stamina and mood stability, making it easier to handle emotional stressors. Engaging in hobbies or activities that bring joy can also serve as powerful emotional buffers during tough transitions.

By incorporating these practices, emotional resilience can become a steady source of strength, helping you maintain balance and purpose during change. Through acceptance, emotional awareness, constructive self-talk, boundaries, support, and self-care, individuals can not only endure transitions but also find pathways for personal growth and fulfilment amid life's inevitable shifts.

5. Building a Support Network for Accountability

During transitions, it's beneficial to surround yourself with a support network that can provide accountability, encouragement, and guidance. Trusted mentors, friends, or colleagues can offer perspective and serve as anchors, helping you stay disciplined even when self-motivation wavers.

Consider the transition of Sundar Pichai to the CEO role at Google. His transition was supported by a network of leaders who guided him, from Larry Page and Sergey Brin to other senior executives. This support system allowed Pichai to navigate complex challenges with confidence, making disciplined decisions aligned with his vision for Google's future.

To build your support network, reach out to individuals who understand your aspirations and can offer constructive feedback. Regular check-ins with these mentors or peers can help keep you accountable and motivated, providing a disciplined framework within which to operate. These relationships often become invaluable assets, particularly when navigating unpredictable or high-stakes changes.

6. Practicing Patience and Persistence

Transitions require patience—an often-overlooked aspect of discipline. When we're eager to see progress or outcomes, it's easy to become discouraged by setbacks or delays. However, successful navigation of life changes often depends on the ability to persist even when immediate results are not visible.

Consider the story of **Sara Blakely**, the founder of Spanx. Before her brand became a global phenomenon, she faced countless rejections from manufacturers who dismissed her innovative idea for shapewear. Despite the setbacks, she remained patient, refining her pitch and persisting in her efforts to bring her vision to life. Eventually, her determination paid off, and Spanx became a multimillion-dollar enterprise. Blakely's story underscores how resilience and perseverance can turn a unique idea into a transformative success.

In your journey, practice patience by setting realistic expectations and reminding yourself that meaningful change takes time. Celebrate small wins along the way, reinforcing your commitment to discipline and persistence. Remember that every step, no matter how small, contributes to the larger journey, and remaining patient is a discipline in itself.

7. Developing a Mindset of Flexibility and Adaptability

While discipline is crucial, flexibility within that discipline is equally important. Life transitions often require us to pivot or adjust our strategies. Being rigid can lead to frustration or burnout; instead, practice adaptable discipline—remaining committed to your goals while being willing to adjust your approach as circumstances evolve.

An apt example of flexibility and adaptability is **Nikhil Kamath**, co-founder of Zerodha, India's largest stockbroking platform. Starting as a high school dropout, Kamath adapted his career trajectory by entering the financial markets and understanding the gaps in India's stockbroking industry. He embraced technology to simplify investing for retail traders and adapted to regulatory changes by continually innovating. During the rise of fintech, Zerodha introduced user-centric platforms, maintaining its leadership. Kamath's ability to foresee market shifts and respond proactively illustrates the power of adaptability in sustaining success.

Incorporate flexibility by periodically reviewing your goals and assessing whether your strategies align with current realities. This approach allows you to adjust your path without compromising your discipline, creating a balanced framework that is both goal-oriented and responsive to change.

Navigating life transitions is a journey that tests and refines our discipline. By embracing change as a growth opportunity, setting clear goals, managing emotions, building a support network, practicing patience, and remaining flexible, you create a foundation that empowers you to face uncertainty with purpose and resolve.

Discipline becomes a stabilizing force, guiding you through each phase with clarity and intention. Whether you're transitioning into a new career, moving to a different city, or embarking on a personal transformation, this disciplined approach will serve as a compass, keeping you aligned with your deeper purpose and propelling you toward a future built on resilience, adaptability, and sustained success.

Every act of discipline strengthens your foundation for a life of achievement

Chapter 10

Sustaining Discipline

Achieving a disciplined purpose isn't a one-time effort. To reach and sustain true success, discipline must evolve into a way of life—a sustained commitment that weathers both success and setbacks. This chapter dives into practical methods, psychological tools, and real-world examples to build and maintain the discipline that fuels long-term growth.

The journey to long-term success often begins with excitement and lofty ambitions, but sustaining this energy requires cultivating self-discipline in a way that evolves with life's changes. Discipline is the foundation of long-term success because it roots our purpose in habits that grow stronger over time. Whether you're a young professional navigating the start of your career, an entrepreneur aiming for sustainable business growth, or an aspiring leader looking for excellence, sustaining discipline is vital.

1. Understanding Sustained Discipline: Beyond Willpower

Many people believe that discipline is only about willpower—a pool we can draw from indefinitely. But studies, especially those in behavioural psychology, reveal that discipline requires more than willpower. Sustained discipline, however, relies on a holistic approach, surpassing sheer willpower, to achieve long-lasting change. Unlike short bursts of self-control, sustained discipline is about creating environments, routines, and mental strategies that naturally reinforce habits, making goals achievable even on low-motivation days. Research in psychology suggests that while willpower is finite and can be depleted, structuring our lives to minimize decision fatigue—by using habits, planning, and environment design—preserves mental energy.

Consider systems thinking as a foundation for sustained discipline: establishing consistent routines and automated behaviours around priority tasks, so they require minimal willpower to perform. By breaking large goals into small, manageable actions, discipline becomes less about resisting temptation and more about intentionally aligning life's activities with core goals. Individuals who prioritize fitness may keep workout equipment readily accessible or schedule exercise during high-energy periods of the day, making it part of their environment rather than solely a test of willpower.

Successful business leaders and high-achievers often focus on creating disciplined systems instead of relying on moment-to-moment willpower. They design routines that focus on decision minimization, practice goal revision, and maintain long-term motivation. This enables sustained discipline, not through constant effort, but through a lifestyle designed to prioritize and protect focus effortlessly.

2. Building Systems for Sustainable Discipline

Discipline thrives when supported by well-designed systems that make consistent action easier and more reliable. These systems act as scaffolding, enabling discipline to become a natural part of daily routines. Whether through setting clear priorities, leveraging tools, or creating accountability mechanisms, building systems ensures that discipline becomes sustainable over time, empowering individuals to stay aligned with their objectives even during challenging periods.

I. Define Non-Negotiables: Sustainable discipline thrives on setting clear priorities—areas in your life that are non-negotiable. This could include health, family time, or core business goals. Non-negotiables create boundaries that keep you grounded. For instance, Azim Premji, the founder of Wipro, has consistently dedicated resources toward education in India as part of his mission to give back. This commitment remains a non-negotiable part of his leadership, reinforcing discipline across his work and philanthropy.

II. *Designing Routine for Predictability:* A robust routine provides structure and predictability, making it easier to maintain discipline. But routines should not be rigid to the point of stifling flexibility. Oprah Winfrey balances a highly structured schedule with flexibility, allowing her to incorporate spontaneity while ensuring that essential tasks are completed.

III. *Utilizing Time-Blocking and Task-Batching:* Techniques like time-blocking and **task-batching*** can help sustain discipline, particularly when juggling multiple responsibilities. By dedicating blocks of time to specific tasks, you reduce task-switching, which conserves mental energy. This technique is used by Elon Musk, who organizes his day in five-minute blocks, ensuring that every minute is purposefully aligned with his goals.

IV. *Harnessing the Power of Small Wins:* While big accomplishments are celebrated, sustainable discipline benefits from recognizing small wins. Small achievements reinforce our sense of progress, motivating us to keep pushing forward. In the context of leadership, small wins could be as simple as having a productive meeting, successfully completing a project milestone, or getting positive feedback from a team member. In the Japanese concept of kaizen, or continuous improvement, the emphasis is on small changes as the foundation for lasting improvement.

Similarly, if you're working on building a new skill, acknowledge every step forward. Suppose your goal is to become more proficient in public speaking. Every time you present confidently to a small group or receive constructive feedback, recognize it as progress.

> ***Task Batching*** *is the practice of grouping similar tasks and completing them in focused blocks of time. This approach minimizes context-switching, which can drain mental energy and reduce efficiency. For example, rather than checking emails intermittently throughout the day, allocate a specific time to handle all correspondence at once. Similarly, creative tasks like content creation or brainstorming can be batched for deeper focus. Task batching fosters productivity by aligning tasks with the brain's natural rhythm, helping you maintain flow and achieve more in less time.*

3. Managing Discouragement and Setbacks

One of the most significant obstacles to sustained discipline is dealing with setbacks. Success is not linear, and setbacks can derail our momentum if we're unprepared to handle them. Here are some strategies to sustain discipline even during challenges:

I. Embrace Setbacks as Learning Moments: Leaders who demonstrate resilience, like Anand Mahindra, chairman of Mahindra Group, often view setbacks as feedback, not failures. When Mahindra Group's electric vehicle venture faced challenges, Mahindra responded by recalibrating its strategy, treating obstacles as learning experiences rather than giving up.

II. Establish a Support Network: Surrounding yourself with supportive people who hold you accountable can help you overcome moments of doubt. In business, this could mean fostering a team culture that supports one another's goals. Outside of work, it could involve family members, friends, or a mentor who can provide encouragement and perspective.

III. Refocus on the Bigger Picture: Sustained discipline requires a clear vision of what you want to achieve and why it matters. Regularly reminding yourself of the big picture can provide the motivation to keep going. Jeff Bezos often attributes Amazon's success to an unwavering focus on long-term goals, even when faced with short-term setbacks.

4. Maintaining Physical and Mental Health

Long-term discipline cannot be sustained without maintaining physical and mental well-being. High performers like Richard

Branson emphasize the role of physical fitness in maintaining energy and focus. Branson often credits his fitness regimen with providing the mental clarity and endurance required to lead Virgin Group through demanding challenges.

I. Physical Health

Physical health is a cornerstone of sustained discipline and optimal performance. Regular exercise, balanced nutrition, and adequate sleep each play a critical role in energy management, mental clarity, and emotional resilience. Exercise, for instance, releases endorphins that improve mood, reduce stress, and enhance cognitive function, directly supporting mental resilience and focus.

Proper nutrition stabilizes energy levels and prevents cognitive fatigue, while sleep is essential for recovery, memory consolidation, and emotional regulation. Leaders and high achievers who prioritize these areas are better equipped to handle stress, make clear decisions, and maintain discipline. Emphasizing physical health ultimately creates a positive feedback loop, where a healthy body supports a disciplined mind, and disciplined actions further support physical well-being.

Incorporating these habits can start small, like a daily walk, gradual improvements to diet, or a consistent bedtime, which eventually build into a holistic lifestyle.

II. Mental Health Practices

Mental health practices are integral to long-term discipline and success. Techniques such as mindfulness, meditation, and cognitive behavioural strategies – such as cognitive restructuring, behavioural activation etc… help in reducing stress, increasing focus, and boosting emotional regulation. Developing a mindset that embraces self-compassion while maintaining a sense of mental clarity is key. Journaling or daily reflections can provide insight into one's emotional state, enabling individuals to address challenges before they become overwhelming.

Leaders and professionals who incorporate regular mental health practices into their routines are better able to handle setbacks, maintain resilience, and remain committed to their goals.

5. Setting Boundaries to Protect Focus

Setting boundaries to protect focus is a key aspect of maintaining sustained discipline. It involves consciously creating space to prioritize important tasks while minimizing distractions. This includes setting limits on how much time you allocate to social media, email, and unnecessary meetings. More importantly, it's about learning to say "no" to requests or activities that don't align with your goals.

Successful leaders and professionals know the importance of carving out dedicated time for deep work. They set clear expectations with colleagues and family members, ensuring their focus remains undisturbed during these periods. Additionally, physical boundaries, such as creating a quiet workspace or using noise-cancelling headphones, can also help reinforce mental boundaries.

Establishing routines that signal the beginning and end of work can help maintain a clear demarcation between work and personal life. By protecting your focus, you can cultivate a sense of discipline that supports long-term success.

Warren Buffet's principle of the "20-slot rule" is a powerful way of setting boundaries. He suggests that individuals should limit themselves to focusing on a small number of priorities, effectively reducing the noise that can disrupt discipline.

6. Leveraging Technology Mindfully

In today's digital age, technology offers tools to support discipline, but it can also be a source of distraction. By using technology mindfully, you can automate routines, streamline workflows, and minimize distractions.

I. Productivity Tools: Tools like task managers, scheduling software, and digital planners can help you structure your day effectively. Leaders use these to ensure they focus on high-priority tasks. However, it's essential to avoid over-reliance on technology; the tools should serve as support, not as the main motivators of discipline.

II. Mindful Digital Use: Cal Newport's philosophy of "digital minimalism" suggests being intentional about technology usage. By choosing tools that align with your goals and eliminating non-essential apps, you can maintain focus and reduce distractions.

7. The Role of Self-Compassion in Sustaining Discipline

Self-compassion is an often-overlooked but essential element in sustaining discipline over the long term. It involves treating yourself with the same kindness and understanding you would offer a friend when you make mistakes or face setbacks. In the pursuit of goals, discipline can sometimes lead to feelings of guilt or frustration when progress stalls or failure occurs. This is where self-compassion becomes vital—it allows you to acknowledge those moments without letting them derail your efforts.

Leaders and high achievers who practice self-compassion can maintain a balanced, sustainable approach to their ambitions. They are better equipped to bounce back from challenges because they aren't weighed down by self-criticism or harsh judgment. Instead, they use setbacks as learning opportunities, maintaining the emotional resilience needed to continue forward.

Moreover, self-compassion fosters emotional well-being by preventing burnout. It helps people remain disciplined by prioritizing mental and physical health, rather than pushing themselves relentlessly at the expense of their well-being. When you're kind to yourself, you reduce the risk of overwhelm and frustration, which could otherwise lead to burnout or abandoning your goals altogether.

The famous entrepreneur Arianna Huffington, emphasizes self-compassion in her wellness philosophy. She credits her ability to keep innovating and managing her numerous ventures to her practice of slowing down, taking breaks, and being kind to herself during tough periods. This helps her recharge and refocus, ultimately sustaining her discipline and drive for long-term success.

For anyone working toward ambitious goals, self-compassion isn't about lowering standards or excusing a lack of discipline; it's about providing the emotional balance needed to stay on course without self-sabotaging behaviour. When you treat yourself with understanding, it becomes easier to return to your tasks with renewed energy and commitment. This practice helps sustain your discipline through the inevitable highs and lows of any long-term pursuit.

Sustaining discipline over the long term involves much more than sheer determination; it's a holistic approach that incorporates physical health, mental resilience, supportive relationships, and adaptable systems. By cultivating sustainable habits, prioritizing well-being, and surrounding yourself with a support network, discipline becomes a reliable, long-term companion in the pursuit of meaningful goals.

With a foundation rooted in purposeful discipline, aspiring leaders, entrepreneurs, and professionals can navigate challenges, seize opportunities, and continue growing into the best versions of themselves.

The disciplined mind sees opportunity where others see excuses

Chapter 11

Emotional Intelligence in Discipline

Emotional Intelligence (EI) and discipline are interconnected, forming a powerful foundation for personal and professional growth. For individuals pursuing a structured path to self-improvement, EI's influence on discipline is both transformative and practical. Emotional intelligence is more than handling emotions; it's about self-awareness, empathy, and social skills that help in managing relationships and fostering resilience in the face of setbacks. When discipline is rooted in strong EI, it becomes adaptable and sustainable, improving focus and making challenging goals achievable.

Imagine an entrepreneur building a business from the ground up. Without EI, the stress, setbacks, and sacrifices could drain their mental energy. But with EI, they maintain discipline not through sheer willpower alone, but through strategic self-regulation, self-awareness, and an ability to empathize with customers and employees. This chapter will explore practical ways that emotional intelligence can support disciplined living and serve as a backbone to one's pursuit of purpose.

1. Understanding the Foundation: Self-Awareness and Self-Regulation

Self-awareness and self-regulation form the essential groundwork for building discipline. They enable individuals to recognize and manage their emotional responses, tendencies, and motivations. This introspective process of understanding ourselves allows us to identify strengths, weaknesses, triggers, and behavioural patterns, which is critical for making consistent, goal-aligned decisions.

I. *Self-Awareness: Knowing One's Inner Landscape*

Self-awareness is the ability to understand one's internal states, preferences, and tendencies. It involves an honest assessment of values, goals, and emotions, providing clarity on what drives actions and choices. This awareness fosters an understanding of how specific situations, environments, or interactions influence mood and behaviour. For instance, if a leader knows they become anxious under time constraints, they can consciously prepare strategies to manage this tendency—whether through time management, mindfulness, or delegation.

Developing self-awareness involves regularly engaging in practices like reflective journaling, meditation, or feedback-seeking from others. Reflective practices allow individuals to observe patterns over time and recognize triggers for emotional responses. For example, journaling can reveal that certain types of challenges motivate a person, while others drain their energy. This knowledge equips them to pursue goals with greater intention, aligning their actions with strengths and preferences.

II. *Self-Regulation: Managing Responses to Enhance Discipline*

Self-regulation is the ability to manage emotions and reactions constructively. It goes hand-in-hand with self-awareness by allowing individuals to pause, process emotions, and choose actions aligned with long-term goals rather than reacting impulsively. High self-regulation is evident in someone who, instead of reacting in anger to criticism, reflects on the feedback and uses it constructively. This practice of pausing and considering options strengthens the foundation of discipline, as it curtails disruptive emotions and fosters a focus on purposeful actions.

A well-known example is Mahatma Gandhi's disciplined approach to advocacy. He demonstrated profound self-regulation, refraining from anger even in extreme adversity, and modelled constructive responses in the face of opposition. This level of self-control enabled him to pursue his goals with unwavering discipline, even under pressure.

Practical ways to develop self-regulation include setting clear intentions, practicing stress-relief techniques (such as breathing exercises or mindfulness), and building mental resilience to handle challenges calmly. Another effective method is **visualization***—envisioning both potential challenges and the response aligned with one's purpose can make it easier to manage reactions in real situations. In high-stress scenarios, people with self-regulation skills are more likely to find productive solutions rather than succumb to stress or impulsive reactions.

III. *Integrating Self-Awareness and Self-Regulation for Discipline*

When self-awareness and self-regulation work in tandem, they create a foundation that supports disciplined actions and decisions. Self-awareness provides insight, and self-regulation enables constructive responses, both of which are critical for aligning with long-term goals. For example, an entrepreneur might realize (through self-awareness) that they often procrastinate on administrative tasks. Using self-regulation, they can then set a structured plan, even employing accountability partners, to ensure these tasks are completed regularly despite any reluctance.

By cultivating self-awareness and self-regulation, individuals build the resilience to pursue challenging goals and maintain a disciplined approach, ultimately leading to more purposeful and sustained success.

Vineet Nayar, CEO of HCL Technologies who led the company through an intense period of growth. Nayar implemented a "Employees First, Customers Second" philosophy, demonstrating a high degree of self-awareness in leadership. He understood that a disciplined organization wasn't simply built through metrics and targets but through emotional engagement with his team, acknowledging that understanding and empowering employees would lead to sustained productivity and innovation. His self-awareness enabled him to foster a culture that valued discipline but through an empathetic, inclusive approach.

Mary Barra, CEO of General Motors, demonstrated this quality as she led the company through multiple crises, including a massive vehicle recall. Barra's ability to self-regulate and stay focused under immense pressure helped her guide GM with a disciplined approach. Rather than reacting defensively, she focused on transparency, owning the problem, and addressing it constructively. Her disciplined response not only restored trust but also set a precedent for GM's values moving forward.

2. Empathy and Social Awareness: Strengthening Discipline Through Relationships

Empathy and social awareness—core components of emotional intelligence—are crucial for building and sustaining discipline in relational contexts. Empathy, the ability to understand and share the feelings of another, and social awareness, recognizing and interpreting social cues, allow leaders to create meaningful connections and respond appropriately in diverse social environments. Together, these qualities can enhance discipline by fostering trust, adaptability, and constructive relationships that align with broader goals.

I. *The Role of Empathy in Strengthening Discipline*

Empathy enhances discipline by enabling individuals to view situations from multiple perspectives, fostering patience, understanding, and the ability to remain composed in challenging interactions. For instance, a leader who empathizes with an underperforming team member may address the situation with curiosity and support rather than frustration. This empathy-driven approach builds trust and can inspire the employee to improve, benefiting the team and reinforcing disciplined, relationship-focused leadership.

Building empathy can be an active practice. Engaging in active listening—focusing intently on what others say, paraphrasing their words, and acknowledging their feelings—can help leaders gain deeper insights into others' motivations and concerns. Practicing empathy also reduces impulsive reactions, as it encourages taking a step back to consider the perspective of others. Over time, this fosters a more disciplined approach to handling interpersonal dynamics.

II. *Social Awareness: Navigating Social Dynamics with Discipline*

Social awareness is the skill of accurately reading the emotional landscape in a group setting. It involves recognizing social cues, group dynamics, and potential sources of tension. Leaders with strong social awareness are attuned to shifts in mood, morale, and motivation within their teams, allowing them to address issues before they escalate. A socially aware manager may notice signs of disengagement in their team after a major organizational change, allowing them to implement strategies to re-engage and reassure the team.

Socially aware leaders use this skill to tailor their communication and actions, creating an environment that feels inclusive and respectful. This attentiveness to context can also help leaders maintain discipline, as they become better equipped to navigate sensitive situations with care, reducing misunderstandings and resistance. To cultivate social awareness, you can observe body language, ask open-ended questions, and regularly seek feedback to understand how they are perceived.

III. *Integrating Empathy and Social Awareness for Disciplined Leadership*

When empathy and social awareness are integrated, they create a foundation for disciplined relationships based on respect and understanding. This foundation is particularly important for leaders managing diverse teams, where varied cultural and personal backgrounds require thoughtful, adaptive approaches. By understanding both the individual needs and broader social dynamics within their teams, leaders can avoid impulsive decisions or responses that could harm relationships or hinder team cohesion.

Satya Nadella, CEO of Microsoft, prioritized empathy as part of Microsoft's cultural transformation, leading to a more collaborative, innovative environment. His empathetic approach enabled Microsoft to retain and attract talent, boost morale, and build a culture that supports both individual growth and collective goals—a testament to how empathy can contribute to disciplined, resilient leadership.

Leaders who consistently practice empathy and social awareness find that their disciplined approach to relationships strengthens team unity, productivity, and commitment to shared objectives. This practice ultimately reinforces their leadership effectiveness and aligns personal discipline with collective success, proving that empathy and social awareness are not just "soft" skills but essential components of sustainable, disciplined leadership.

3. Motivation and Self-Determination: Sustaining Discipline Over Time

Emotional intelligence fuels the motivation required to maintain disciplined habits. While intrinsic motivation—the drive that comes from within—is ideal for sustaining discipline, it must be consciously nurtured. EQ helps individuals tap into this inner motivation by aligning actions with values and purpose, making discipline less about obligation and more about commitment.

Real-world examples abound of leaders who exemplify motivation rooted in self-awareness and purpose. A prominent Indian example is late Ratan Tata, former chairman of Tata Group, who demonstrated discipline throughout his tenure by constantly aligning his business practices with a strong sense of social responsibility. Tata's disciplined approach to expanding Tata Group was not driven purely by profits but by a vision of ethical leadership and societal impact, creating motivation that extended beyond business goals to a larger purpose.

By recognizing the "why" behind their goals, individuals are less likely to be swayed by distractions and more inclined to persevere when faced with setbacks. Building a habit of reflecting on core motivations can help sustain discipline through prolonged effort. Emotional intelligence provides a framework for understanding what fuels personal and professional ambitions, ensuring that discipline remains anchored in meaningful objectives.

4. Handling Stress and Building Resilience: The Role of EI in Discipline

In the pursuit of challenging goals, stress is inevitable. Emotional intelligence equips individuals with tools to manage stress constructively, preventing it from undermining discipline. Resilience, a critical component of EI, is especially important in the face of failure or unexpected challenges, allowing disciplined habits to persist even when the path forward is unclear.

Angela Merkel has demonstrated resilience through disciplined EI. Merkel's tenure as Germany's chancellor saw numerous crises, yet her ability to remain calm, analyse situations thoroughly, and make disciplined decisions has been widely praised. Merkel's resilience is rooted in her ability to manage emotions effectively, respond to pressure calmly, and maintain a disciplined approach to governance—even under extreme circumstances. Her approach to leadership underlines how EQ-driven resilience can enable disciplined responses in the most challenging environments.

Similarly, the concept of resilience can be applied in everyday professional life, whether it's dealing with demanding projects, tight deadlines, or interpersonal conflicts. Practicing resilience through a balanced perspective and disciplined problem-solving builds an enduring form of discipline that can withstand various pressures. Emotional intelligence ensures that resilience is not merely reactive but pre-emptive, helping individuals anticipate challenges and develop coping mechanisms that support long-term success.

5. Practical Techniques for Integrating EI with Discipline

Integrating emotional intelligence with discipline is a skill that requires consistent practice. Here are a few practical methods to enhance EI's influence on disciplined living:

I. *Regular Self-Reflection*: Allocate time for daily or weekly self-reflection. Use journaling or meditation to assess emotions, recognize triggers, and review progress on disciplined habits. By staying connected to inner experiences, self-reflection fosters greater self-awareness, ensuring that discipline remains aligned with one's values.

II. *Mindfulness Practices*: Mindfulness improves self-regulation by helping individuals remain present and composed, reducing impulsivity. Simple techniques such as deep breathing or mindfulness meditation can aid in grounding oneself, particularly in high-stress situations.

III. *Empathy Exercises*: Practice empathy by regularly placing yourself in others' perspectives. In team settings, actively seek feedback and listen without judgment. Empathy improves collaboration and encourages disciplined communication, which is essential for sustaining focused, productive relationships.

IV. *Goal Visualization and Motivation Alignment*: Visualize long-term goals and identify the core motivations behind them. Aligning discipline with intrinsic motivation creates resilience and reduces reliance on external rewards, making disciplined actions feel rewarding in themselves.

V. *Stress-Management Techniques*: Develop a toolkit for managing stress, including exercise, hobbies, and healthy social interactions. By building coping mechanisms, stress becomes more manageable, supporting disciplined habits even under pressure.

VI. Conflict Resolution Skills: Cultivate communication skills to address conflicts constructively. Approaching disagreements with empathy and self-regulation strengthens relationships and fosters a disciplined approach to problem-solving.

Emotional intelligence is not just an asset but a necessity for disciplined living. By fostering self-awareness, self-regulation, empathy, motivation, and resilience, EQ becomes the backbone of sustainable discipline. Whether pursuing career success, building personal relationships, or achieving personal transformation, the blend of EQ and discipline empowers individuals to remain steadfast and adaptable in a rapidly changing world.

In today's complex landscape, where agility, empathy, and purpose are more important than ever, integrating EQ with discipline allows individuals to navigate challenges without losing sight of their goals. Leaders and aspiring professionals alike will find that emotional intelligence, when practiced alongside disciplined habits, transforms life's path from a series of obstacles to a rewarding journey of growth, resilience, and lasting success.

Visualization:

Visualization exercises are powerful tools for setting and achieving goals. Here's a step-by-step *guide on how to conduct these exercises effectively:*

i. ***Set a Purpose:*** *Identify the specific goal or outcome you want to visualize, such as a career achievement, a successful presentation, or personal growth.*

ii. ***Create a Quiet Space:*** *Choose a comfortable, quiet environment to minimize distractions. Sit or lie down in a relaxed position.*

iii. ***Use Deep Breathing:*** *Start with a few minutes of deep, mindful breathing to centre yourself. This helps calm the mind and prepares it for focus.*

iv. ***Build the Mental Picture:*** *Imagine yourself in the future, having already achieved your goal. Picture the environment, sounds, colours, and sensations in vivid detail. Engage all your senses to make the experience as real as possible.*

v. ***Add Emotion:*** *Feel the emotions associated with success. Emotions like pride, joy, and confidence reinforce the experience, making it more impactful.*

vi. ***Visualize Steps, Not Just Outcomes:*** *Imagine not only the final result but also the steps you'll take to get there. This mental rehearsal can make actual tasks feel more familiar and achievable.*

vii. ***Stay Consistent:*** *Practice visualization regularly, ideally daily. Consistent practice enhances clarity and reinforces commitment to your goal.*

viii. ***Finish with Affirmations:*** *End with positive affirmations or statements that reinforce your belief in achieving the goal.*

Visualization can improve focus, reduce stress, and increase resilience by mentally preparing you for challenges along the journey.

Creating a Personal Success Map:

Creating a Personal Success Map involves charting a path from where you currently are to where you want to be. Here's a guide to building one:

i. ***Clarify Your Vision:*** *Start by identifying your long-term vision—what success looks like to you. This includes your values, desired lifestyle, and achievements.*

ii. ***Set Specific, Measurable Goals:*** *Break your vision down into specific goals (personal, professional, financial, etc.), ensuring they are SMART (Specific, Measurable, Achievable, Relevant, Time-bound).*

iii. ***Identify Key Milestones:*** *Break each goal into smaller, actionable steps. These milestones represent significant moments or achievements on your journey.*

iv. ***Create a Timeline:*** *Establish a realistic timeline for completing each step. Be mindful of your current commitments and resources.*

v. ***Develop an Action Plan:*** *For each milestone, identify the actions required, skills needed, and potential obstacles. Develop strategies to overcome challenges.*

vi. ***Review and Adjust:*** *Regularly track your progress and reflect. Modify your goals or actions, if necessary, based on any shifts in your situation or priorities.*

vii. ***Include a Personal Growth Component:*** *Incorporate aspects of personal development like building discipline, improving emotional intelligence, or expanding your network.*

viii. ***Visualize Your Map:*** *Use a visual tool like a mind map or a flowchart to display your Success Map. This helps with clarity and focus, and it makes the journey feel more tangible.*

ix. ***Celebrate Progress:*** *Recognize and celebrate milestones as you achieve them. Acknowledging progress motivates you to stay on course.*

x. **Stay Flexible:** *Life changes, so your map should be adaptable. Be prepared to update your goals or action steps as you learn more about yourself or face new circumstances.*

Your Personal Success Map serves as both a practical tool for goal-setting and a motivating reminder of the path you're on.

A purpose-driven life isn't just about reaching a goal; it's about becoming who you're meant to be

Chapter 12

Discipline in Leadership and Influence

Discipline is a cornerstone of effective leadership, the backbone that supports consistency, vision, and credibility. In the journey of leading others—whether in a business, community, or personal capacity—discipline transforms a leader's vision from mere intention into impactful action. Discipline in leadership is not about rigid control but a balanced dedication to one's commitments, values, and influence. For aspiring leaders, young professionals, and entrepreneurs alike, it is a fundamental tool to inspire trust and create a sustainable impact.

Effective leadership rooted in discipline becomes a form of influence that resonates with people at all levels.

A disciplined leader is focused yet flexible, committed yet adaptive, guiding people with clarity, resilience, and unwavering purpose. Discipline in leadership means applying consistent standards and holding oneself accountable, even in the face of challenges.

Let's explore how discipline in leadership and influence unfolds practically, examining key strategies, real-world examples, and actionable insights to help aspiring leaders develop a disciplined approach.

1. The Foundation of Disciplined Leadership: Values and Vision

A leader's discipline is deeply tied to their personal values and long-term vision. True discipline stems from an unwavering belief in a purpose larger than oneself, guiding every decision and action. This alignment between values and actions forms the bedrock of trust. When employees, peers, and stakeholders see leaders acting consistently with their values, respect follows naturally.

Falguni Nayar, the founder and CEO of Nykaa, showcases disciplined leadership shaped by a clear vision and strong values. Leaving behind a successful career in investment banking, she pursued her vision of creating a premium online beauty and wellness platform tailored to Indian consumers. With a disciplined focus on customer experience, authenticity, and innovation, Nayar transformed

Nykaa into a market leader. Her values of perseverance, inclusivity, and building trust with stakeholders have been instrumental in making Nykaa a globally recognized brand, inspiring entrepreneurs to dream big while staying true to their principles.

For aspiring leaders, this example underlines the importance of identifying and embracing values that resonate personally and professionally. With clarity in values, leaders can maintain a disciplined approach that consistently guides their actions, even when facing difficult choices.

2. Setting a Standard and Leading by Example

Leaders who embody discipline set a high standard for their teams. Leaders shape organizational culture and employee behaviour by demonstrating their commitment to shared values through their actions. Setting a standard means embodying the principles a leader wants their team to adopt, serving as a benchmark for integrity, discipline, and accountability. This behaviour provides a consistent point of reference for employees, making expectations clear and more likely to be adopted at every level.

During his tenure as CEO of Unilever, Paul Polman exemplified the power of leading by example. He shifted the company's focus from quarterly earnings to long-term sustainability, rejecting short-termism and stressing that business could succeed by contributing to society. Under

Polman's guidance, Unilever launched the Sustainable Living Plan, which aimed to reduce the company's environmental impact while improving the lives of people across its supply chain. By making bold public commitments, such as cutting greenhouse gas emissions and improving worker conditions, Polman demonstrated his principles through Unilever's actions, setting a powerful example in the corporate world.

I. How Leading by Example Drives Accountability and Discipline: When leaders set high standards through their actions, it cultivates a disciplined environment where everyone feels accountable. Employees understand that leadership isn't expecting anything they wouldn't do themselves. This approach can be seen in companies where leaders engage directly in both challenges and opportunities. A CEO who actively supports sustainability by adopting green office policies not only shows commitment but also makes employees more likely to follow suit.

II. Cultivating Resilience and Ethical Decision-Making: Setting a standard also involves navigating ethical dilemmas transparently. When leaders consistently choose the ethical path, they encourage their teams to prioritize long-term integrity over short-term gains. This practice strengthens the organization's resilience and improves decision-making processes at all levels.

In practice, leaders who set a strong standard create a foundation for sustained discipline and accountability across the organization. By aligning actions with values and demonstrating an unwavering commitment to these principles, leaders inspire their teams to follow, creating a cohesive, values-driven culture.

For young professionals and aspiring leaders, adopting this mindset means not only setting high standards for yourself but also practicing self-accountability. Even small actions, like meeting deadlines consistently or delivering quality work under pressure, build the habit of discipline that others can observe and respect.

3. Consistency in Action: Building Trust and Credibility

Consistency is the essence of disciplined leadership. Consistency in action is a cornerstone of building trust and credibility in leadership. Leaders who consistently align their actions with their words demonstrate reliability, fostering an environment where employees feel secure and confident in the leadership's direction. This consistency ensures that employees are not second-guessing or questioning motives; rather, they see a leader who is predictable in their values and decisions.

I. Trust Through Dependability: When leaders are predictable and consistent, they create a dependable foundation. For instance, if a leader emphasizes the importance of work-life balance but regularly expects after-hours communication, it can erode trust. But a leader who respects boundaries, models balance, and values employee well-being builds a trustworthy rapport.

II. *Reinforcing Company Values*: Consistency serves as a reinforcement of core values. A leader who regularly upholds values like integrity, customer focus, or innovation through disciplined actions provides a living example of what the organization stands for. This alignment not only strengthens trust but also embeds those values in the organization's culture, as employees take cues from leadership's repeated behaviours.

III. *Credibility in Decision-Making*: Consistency in decision-making also boosts credibility, as leaders are seen to apply principles with disciplined uniformity, even in challenging situations. Howard Schultz of Starbucks focused on employee benefits even during downturns, proving his commitment to employees, which fostered loyalty and trust in his leadership. By sticking to principles and not wavering based on convenience, leaders reinforce their credibility, establishing a fair and transparent culture.

IV. *Long-term Impact*: Over time, consistent, disciplined leadership builds an unshakeable foundation of trust, which is crucial during times of uncertainty. Employees are more likely to remain engaged, motivated, and loyal when they know they can rely on their leader to act in a steady, predictable manner, regardless of circumstances. This trust creates a resilient culture that can weather adversity and thrive through change.

In essence, consistency is not only about following through on commitments; it's about embodying a set of principles that employees can trust. Through small, everyday actions and major organizational decisions alike, leaders who are consistent in their actions create a legacy of credibility that strengthens the entire organization.

For leaders today, particularly those in dynamic or unstable industries, maintaining a consistent approach may be challenging. However, by upholding a disciplined consistency in their vision, tone, and actions, leaders can build a foundation of trust that withstands fluctuations in the external environment.

4. Communication Discipline: Clear, Transparent, and Authentic

Effective leaders recognize the critical role of disciplined communication in building trust, clarity, and alignment within an organization. By ensuring their messaging is clear, transparent, and authentic, they create a foundation of openness and reliability that resonates deeply with teams and stakeholders alike.

I. *Clarity: Eliminating Ambiguity*

Clear communication is essential in providing direction, setting expectations, and minimizing misunderstandings. Leaders who are disciplined in clarity focus on eliminating jargon, simplifying complex ideas, and making sure their message reaches everyone in a way that's easy to understand. This means being specific about goals, timelines, and outcomes, which helps teams work in sync and stay aligned with the organization's vision. Amazon founder Jeff Bezos is known for his emphasis on clarity in communication. His insistence on writing clear, in-depth memos for meetings encourages thoughtful discussion and reduces the risk of misalignment.

II. *Transparency: Building Trust Through Openness*

Transparency in communication means being honest about both successes and setbacks. Leaders who are disciplined in transparency regularly update their teams on the organization's progress and are open about challenges, fostering an environment of trust. This openness reduces speculation and the spread of misinformation, empowering employees to make informed decisions and remain focused. For instance, Satya Nadella at Microsoft exemplified transparency when transforming the company's culture. He openly and regularly communicated the need for a shift from a "know-it-all" to a "learn-it-all" mindset, aligning employees around a shared purpose of growth and innovation.

III. *Authenticity: Staying True to Core Values*

Authenticity in communication builds emotional connections with teams, encouraging loyalty and commitment. Authentic leaders, communicate with genuine intention and stay true to their core values, even in difficult situations. Authenticity includes sharing personal insights, admitting mistakes, and being approachable, which fosters an inclusive culture. Howard Schultz, former CEO of Starbucks, demonstrated this by frequently sharing his personal journey and values with employees, emphasizing his commitment to creating a "third place" that respects employees and customers alike. His authentic approach helped embed a customer-first and employee-centric ethos at Starbucks.

IV. *Practicing Communication Discipline Consistently*

Discipline in communication also means being regular and consistent with updates. Leaders who schedule regular touchpoints, such as weekly briefings or town hall meetings, demonstrate a commitment to keeping their teams informed. Consistent communication prevents information gaps and provides a predictable structure that teams can rely on. During the COVID-19 pandemic, leaders at several companies, used social media and internal channels to provide frequent updates, sharing both operational changes and support measures. This not only helped manage employee concerns but also kept morale high.

V. *Impact of Disciplined Communication on Organizational Culture*

When leaders practice disciplined communication—balancing clarity, transparency, and authenticity—they create a culture of accountability and engagement. Employees feel empowered to speak up, provide feedback, and contribute ideas, knowing their input is valued in an environment where open dialogue is encouraged. Disciplined communication fosters a cycle of continuous improvement, as feedback and information flow freely within the organization.

In essence, communication discipline requires leaders to go beyond simply delivering a message. It involves ensuring that every interaction is intentional, thoughtfully crafted, and aligned with the organization's values. By maintaining clarity, transparency, and authenticity, leaders cultivate a culture of trust and openness, which ultimately strengthens relationships and drives long-term success.

Disciplined communication means preparing thoughtfully, being transparent, and maintaining honesty even in difficult conversations. This approach inspires trust and encourages others to adopt a similar open communication style.

5. Developing a Discipline of Continuous Learning

Continuous learning is a cornerstone of sustained leadership excellence in a rapidly changing world. Leaders who commit to lifelong discipline of learning remain adaptable, relevant, and resilient, able to lead their teams effectively through new challenges. The discipline of continuous learning extends beyond formal education and includes real-world experiences, feedback, mentorship, and self-reflection. This approach cultivates agility, fosters innovation, and helps leaders stay on the cutting edge of industry trends.

I. *Embracing a Growth Mindset*

A disciplined approach to learning starts with adopting a growth mindset, as popularized by psychologist **Carol Dweck**. Leaders with this mindset view challenges and setbacks as opportunities to grow rather than as failures. This shift in perspective encourages experimentation and calculated risk-taking, which are vital in leadership. Sundar Pichai, CEO of Alphabet Inc., is known for his commitment to a growth mindset, often encouraging his teams to think big and innovate beyond traditional limits.

II. *Setting Learning Goals*

To make continuous learning sustainable, it's essential to set specific, actionable learning goals. Leaders can start by identifying areas that align with their professional responsibilities and areas for personal development. These goals might include staying current with industry innovations, improving interpersonal skills, or learning about new fields that could impact their organization. Establishing short- and long-term learning objectives creates a roadmap, making it easier to measure progress and stay motivated.

III. *Leveraging Diverse Learning Sources*

The discipline of learning isn't confined to traditional methods. Leaders today have access to a multitude of learning formats, including online courses, podcasts, industry conferences, and networking opportunities. Engaging with diverse perspectives: from industry peers, thought leaders, and innovators; broadens understanding and can provide practical insights.

IV. *Learning Through Feedback*

Feedback serves as an invaluable tool in the learning process, allowing leaders to gain insights into their strengths and areas for growth. Leaders who actively seek feedback—whether from peers, team members, or mentors—demonstrate humility and a commitment to self-improvement. This feedback loop encourages accountability and continuous refinement of leadership style. Bill Gates, co-founder of Microsoft, famously prioritized feedback and welcomed honest critiques as a means of personal and professional growth.

V. *Embracing Failure as a Learning Opportunity*

Discipline in continuous learning involves an acceptance of failure as an inevitable aspect of growth. Leaders who see failure as a learning opportunity are more likely to experiment, innovate, and ultimately succeed. By cultivating resilience and extracting lessons from setbacks, leaders model adaptability for their teams. Elon Musk's journey with SpaceX is a prime example; despite multiple failures in early rocket launches, he used these setbacks to refine and improve, eventually achieving groundbreaking success.

VI. *Prioritizing Reflective Practices*

Reflection is a key part of disciplined learning. By dedicating time to reflect on experiences, leaders gain insights that help refine their strategies and actions. Daily journaling, post-project reviews, or weekly reflections on decisions made and lessons learned can solidify these insights. This reflective discipline not only promotes self-awareness but also allows leaders to recognize patterns, avoid repeated mistakes, and strengthen decision-making.

VII. *Balancing Learning with Application*

Learning must translate into action to be valuable. Leaders who apply new knowledge and skills demonstrate their commitment to growth and inspire their teams to do the same. They experiment with newly acquired skills in real-world situations, assess outcomes, and adjust as needed. For instance, Jack Welch, former CEO of GE, was known for his "learn-and-apply" philosophy, which involved regularly updating skills and applying them immediately in decision-making.

VIII. *Creating a Culture of Learning*

To promote continuous learning at an organizational level, leaders must foster an environment that encourages curiosity and exploration. When leaders share what they learn and celebrate learning achievements within the organization, they inspire a culture of growth. This approach can transform organizations, making them more innovative and agile. Rajesh Gopinathan, CEO TCS has championed a continuous learning culture, emphasizing reskilling and up-skilling to keep pace with rapid technological change.

IX. *Consistency in Learning Efforts*

The true test of disciplined learning is consistency. Developing a habit of learning, even in small, regular doses, builds momentum. Leaders who make learning a non-negotiable part of their routine—whether through reading daily, engaging in regular courses, or setting aside time for reflection—ensure that their knowledge and skills remain sharp.

A disciplined approach to continuous learning equips leaders with the adaptability, resilience, and foresight necessary to navigate an ever-changing landscape. This commitment to growth and self-improvement not only enhances their personal effectiveness but also empowers those around them, creating a culture where innovation and excellence can flourish.

6. Integrity and Ethical Discipline: The Pillars of Lasting Influence

Integrity is the ultimate test of disciplined leadership. While competence and skills can command respect, only ethical behaviour can build lasting influence. Leaders who uphold high ethical standards demonstrate a rare form of discipline—one that often requires resisting short-term gains for long-term trust.

One of the most celebrated examples of ethical discipline is Warren Buffett, CEO of Berkshire Hathaway. Buffett's commitment to ethical investing, his transparency with shareholders, and his decision to avoid risky financial practices have established him as a leader of integrity. His disciplined approach to ethics has not only built Berkshire Hathaway's credibility but has also set a standard in the finance industry.

For any leader, ethical discipline may involve making difficult choices, but it lays the foundation for sustainable influence. Aspiring leaders should remember that in the long run, ethical discipline will create far more substantial rewards than short-term compromises.

7. The Discipline of Empowering Others

A truly disciplined leader understands that empowering others amplifies influence. Disciplined empowerment means giving people autonomy, building trust, and nurturing potential. Leaders who empower their teams create a culture of shared responsibility and collective discipline, enabling everyone to perform at their best.

Indra Nooyi, former CEO of PepsiCo, epitomized this approach. She implemented a strategy called "Performance with Purpose," emphasizing sustainability and ethical responsibility while empowering employees to take ownership of these values. Her disciplined commitment to employee empowerment not only strengthened PepsiCo's brand but also transformed its internal culture, making it more resilient and forward-looking.

Empowering others with discipline involves trusting team members with responsibilities, offering guidance without micromanaging, and providing resources for growth. By doing so, leaders create a ripple effect of disciplined, self-motivated teams.

Discipline in leadership is not a rigid formula but a dynamic and multi-faceted quality. Leaders who adopt a disciplined approach to their values, standards, communication, emotional resilience, learning, ethics, and empowerment set themselves apart. These qualities create a robust framework that can navigate change, inspire trust, and amplify influence. For aspiring leaders, this disciplined approach offers a clear path toward impactful, resilient, and ethical leadership.

Purpose fuels passion and turns ordinary efforts into extraordinary outcomes

Chapter 13

Integrating Discipline with Creativity and Innovation

What comes to mind when you hear the words *creativity* and *discipline*? For many, these concepts seem like polar opposites. Creativity is often associated with freedom, spontaneity, and thinking outside the box. Discipline, on the other hand, is linked to structure, rules, and a systematic approach. At first glance, they appear to contradict each other, as if one stifles the other. However, in reality, the most successful individuals and organizations prove that true brilliance lies in integrating these two forces.

Creativity without discipline is like a spark without fuel—it may dazzle briefly but fails to sustain itself. Similarly, discipline without creativity is like a well-organized machine producing predictable outcomes but lacking innovation or growth. When combined, discipline becomes the framework that nurtures creativity, and creativity adds dynamism and freshness to disciplined efforts. Together, they form a powerful duo that drives meaningful progress and extraordinary success.

Think of some of the greatest achievements in human history—the construction of the Taj Mahal, the moon landing, or the advent of the internet. Behind each of these milestones lies a remarkable interplay of imagination and order. Visionary ideas sparked these endeavours, but disciplined execution turned them into reality.

This chapter delves into the vital relationship between discipline and creativity, showing how they complement and enhance one another. You'll discover how discipline fosters the right environment for creative thinking and how creativity breathes life into disciplined processes. Whether you're an artist striving to complete your next masterpiece, a leader tasked with solving complex challenges, or simply someone seeking to live a more purposeful life, this chapter will help you unlock the combined power of discipline and creativity. You'll learn that, when harmonized, these seemingly opposing forces, can take your potential to unimaginable heights.

1. The Myth: Creativity is Spontaneous

The idea that creativity is purely spontaneous is one of the most enduring myths about the creative process. Popular culture often glorifies the image of the lone genius struck by a sudden flash of inspiration—Newton discovering gravity under an apple tree or Mozart composing symphonies effortlessly. While these stories may hold some truth, they only tell part of the story. The reality is far less glamorous yet far more empowering: creativity is not magic, but a skill that can be cultivated, and it thrives on preparation, persistence, and process.

I. Creativity as a Process, Not an Accident

Creativity is often perceived as an unpredictable force, but most successful creative endeavours follow a disciplined process. Legendary artist Pablo Picasso once said, "Inspiration exists, but it has to find you working." This statement encapsulates the reality of creativity—it emerges most often when you are actively engaged in your craft.

II. The Reality Behind "Sudden Inspiration"

When people describe moments of sudden inspiration, what they often overlook is the countless hours of preparation and effort that preceded those moments. Take the famous story of Isaac Newton and the falling apple. While the apple may have triggered his thoughts on gravity, Newton had already spent years studying mathematics, motion, and physics. The moment of insight was not an isolated event but the culmination of disciplined learning and exploration.

Similarly, The Beatles' music revolutionized the music industry not because of overnight genius but because of relentless practice. Before they became household names, they spent years performing in clubs in Hamburg, Germany, playing for hours each night. This disciplined routine honed their skills, allowing their creativity to flourish.

2. The Neuroscience of Creativity

From a neurological perspective, creativity isn't a random spark but the result of complex interactions in the brain. Neuroscientists have identified key networks involved in creative thinking:

- **The Default Mode Network (DMN):** This is activated during daydreaming and helps generate new ideas.
- **The Executive Control Network (ECN):** This is activated during focused attention, helping refine and execute ideas.
- **The Salience Network:** This acts as a bridge, deciding which ideas are worth pursuing.

To foster creativity, these networks must work together. This doesn't happen by accident—it requires a mix of focus, practice, and reflection, all of which are cultivated through discipline.

3. Creativity in the Professional World

In professional settings, creativity rarely appears out of nowhere. Teams that consistently innovate often follow structured processes to foster creativity. Take Pixar, for example. Known for its groundbreaking films, Pixar doesn't rely on random bursts of inspiration. Instead, they use a disciplined process called the "Braintrust."

During Braintrust sessions, filmmakers present their work to a group of trusted peers for candid feedback. This iterative process ensures that every story idea is tested, refined, and improved. Far from stifling creativity, this disciplined approach enhances it, resulting in some of the most beloved animated films of all time.

Why the Spontaneity Myth Persists

The misconception that creativity is spontaneous persists for several reasons:

I. **Survivor Bias:** We often hear success stories after the fact, without understanding the disciplined effort behind them.

II. **Romanticism:** The notion of effortless genius appeals to our love of myths and legends.

III. **Fear of Effort:** Many people prefer to believe that creativity is a gift they don't have, rather than a skill they can work to develop.

Understanding the truth about creativity - that it requires hard work and persistence - empowers us to take control of our own creative potential.

How Discipline Unlocks Creativity

I. **Routine Generates Momentum:**

Great creators like Maya Angelou and Haruki Murakami followed strict daily routines. Angelou rented a hotel room every day to write, regardless of inspiration. Murakami followed a disciplined schedule of writing, running, and reading. Their adherence to routine created the conditions for creativity to thrive.

II. **Constraints Spark Ingenuity:**

Ironically, limitations can enhance creativity by forcing us to think outside the box. When faced with a low budget, a tight timeline, or limited resources, people often come up with their most innovative solutions. A classic example is the Apollo 13 mission, where NASA engineers used a disciplined approach to solve a life-threatening problem with the materials available on board.

III. Persistence Breeds Mastery:

Malcolm Gladwell's "10,000-hour rule" highlights the connection between disciplined practice and mastery. Whether in art, music, science, or business, the path to innovation often involves putting in the time to refine your skills and ideas.

Shifting the Paradigm

Once you move past the misconception that creativity is purely spontaneous, you unlock a new level of potential. Recognizing that creativity is a process allows you to take control, to cultivate it intentionally, and to pair it with discipline for maximum impact.

As author Elizabeth Gilbert wrote in *Big Magic*, "Don't wait for inspiration to strike. Instead, summon it by showing up." Creativity isn't a gift reserved for the lucky few—it's a skill you can nurture through deliberate action, persistence, and a willingness to keep showing up.

4. Finding the Balance Between Discipline and Creativity

Balancing discipline with creativity may seem challenging at first. Too much structure can stifle innovation, while too little can lead to chaos. The most impactful accomplishments and innovations emerge when these two forces coexist harmoniously. Striking the right balance between discipline and creativity is essential for producing meaningful and sustainable results, whether in art, business, science, or personal growth.

This balance is not about giving equal weight to both at all times but understanding when to lean into discipline and when to embrace creativity. Finding this equilibrium can unlock potential that is greater than the sum of its parts.

Why Balance Matters

Excessive reliance on discipline can stifle innovation. A rigid adherence to rules, procedures, or schedules can create a tunnel vision that limits your ability to think outside the box. While discipline ensures consistency and productivity, it can also lead to burnout or mediocrity if it doesn't allow room for fresh ideas and flexibility.

For instance, companies that prioritize strict processes without fostering innovation risk becoming obsolete. Kodak, once a giant in photography, failed to adapt to the digital revolution because it clung too tightly to its established way of doing business.

On the other hand, unrestrained creativity can lead to chaos. Without a framework to ground the ideas on, creative endeavours may remain unfinished, impractical, or overly ambitious. The excitement of brainstorming and ideations can quickly fizzle out without the focus and consistency that discipline provides.

The intersection of discipline and creativity is where magic happens. Discipline provides the foundation for creative exploration, while creativity injects vitality and innovation into disciplined efforts. Together, they enable you to dream big and act systematically to achieve those dreams.

5. Real-World Examples of Balance

I. Steve Jobs and Apple

Steve Jobs exemplified the harmonious blend of discipline and creativity. He was a visionary who dreamed of revolutionizing technology but also an exacting leader who demanded perfection in execution. The development of the iPhone is a testament to this balance—an innovative product meticulously designed and rigorously tested to ensure functionality and elegance.

Jobs understood that creativity needed structure to thrive. Apple's product development process is famously disciplined, with clear timelines, iterative feedback loops, and uncompromising attention to detail. This blend of creativity and discipline has made Apple a global leader in innovation.

II. Michelangelo and the Sistine Chapel

Michelangelo's creation of the Sistine Chapel ceiling demonstrates how discipline can coexist with artistic creativity. Painting the frescoes was a monumental task that required both technical precision as well as artistic genius. Michelangelo spent years meticulously planning, sketching, and executing his vision, working within the constraints of architecture, theology, and patron demands.

Without discipline, his creativity might have remained limited to ideas or incomplete sketches. By combining structure with inspiration, Michelangelo created a masterpiece that continues to inspire centuries later.

III. IDEO's Design Thinking Process

IDEO, a renowned design firm, integrates discipline with creativity through its design thinking methodology. Their process involves clearly defined stages—empathize, define, ideate, prototype, and test. While these stages provide a disciplined framework, the ideation phase encourages freewheeling creativity, and the prototyping phase emphasizes iterative experimentation.

This balance ensures that innovative ideas are not only generated but also refined into practical solutions that meet user needs.

Balancing discipline and creativity is not about compromise but synergy. When you embrace both, you create a dynamic cycle where creativity generates ideas, and discipline transforms them into reality. This balance fuels growth, innovation, and fulfilment in every area of life.

As you seek to integrate discipline and creativity, remember that the journey is as important as the destination. The process of learning, experimenting, and refining is itself a creative act, one that shapes not only your work but also your character. By finding your balance, you'll unlock the ability to create with purpose and execute with passion—truly building a life of disciplined purpose.

6. Practical Strategies for Integrating Discipline with Creativity

I. Understand Your Natural Tendencies

Begin by assessing whether you naturally lean more toward discipline or creativity. If you're highly disciplined, you may need to consciously make space for exploration and experimentation. If you're more creative, you may need to introduce structure to channel your ideas into actionable outcomes.

Reflection Exercise:

- What are your biggest strengths—creativity or discipline?
- Where do you struggle most—structured execution or freeform ideation?
- Understanding these tendencies is the first step to achieving balance.

II. Set Flexible Boundaries

Discipline doesn't have to mean rigidity. Establish routines and goals that provide a structure but allow for flexibility. For example, allocate specific times for brainstorming, during which all ideas are welcome, no matter how unconventional. Follow this with a disciplined process for evaluating and refining those ideas.

Practical Tip: Use tools like time-blocking for creative and disciplined tasks. Dedicate mornings to freeform idea generation and afternoons to focused execution.

III. Embrace Constraints

Contrary to popular belief, constraints often boost creativity rather than hinder it. Boundaries force you to think outside the box and come up with innovative solutions. For example, when NASA engineers faced the challenge of fixing Apollo 13 with limited materials onboard, their creativity soared under the constraints, saving the astronauts' lives.

In your own life, set deliberate constraints to spark creativity:

- Limit resources to force innovative thinking.
- Set tight deadlines to encourage quick decision-making.

IV. Use Tools to Track Progress

Creativity can feel intangible, but discipline makes it measurable. Use tools like journals, apps, or project management software to track your progress. Keeping a record of ideas and their outcomes helps refine your creative process and ensures consistency.

V. Collaborate with Diverse Thinkers

Innovation often happens at the intersection of different disciplines. Collaborating with individuals who bring unique perspectives can amplify creativity. For example, Steve Jobs believed that Apple's success came from blending technology with the arts, resulting in intuitive and aesthetically pleasing products.

VI. Iterate and Refine

Creativity and discipline thrive in iterative cycles. Begin with creative exploration, generate multiple ideas, and then switch to a disciplined phase of evaluation and refinement. This approach prevents you from getting stuck in endless brainstorming or rigid perfectionism.

7. Real-World Examples of Discipline and Creativity in Action

- **J.K. Rowling: Writing with Purpose and Process**

J.K. Rowling's journey to writing the *Harry Potter* series exemplifies the integration of discipline with creativity. She wrote her first draft while struggling financially, relying on strict routines to bring her vision to life. Despite numerous rejections from publishers, her disciplined approach and belief in her story eventually led to one of the most successful literary franchises in history.

- **Elon Musk: Innovating with Relentless Focus**

Elon Musk's ability to lead companies like Tesla and SpaceX stems from his disciplined approach to problem-solving. At SpaceX, Musk's team faced immense challenges when designing reusable rockets. By adhering to strict timelines, testing rigorously, and constantly refining designs, they achieved breakthroughs that revolutionized space exploration.

- **Pixar: The Marriage of Creativity and Process**

Pixar's success lies in its disciplined creative process. Each movie undergoes a rigorous development cycle, with ideas being tested, critiqued, and improved. Pixar's Braintrust sessions, where teams provide honest feedback on storyboards, ensure that creativity is paired with a structured approach to producing exceptional films.

8. Overcoming Common Challenges

- **"I Don't Feel Inspired Today"**

It's a sentiment we've all experienced—those days when inspiration feels elusive, and motivation seems to have taken a vacation. But the truth is, waiting for inspiration is like waiting for perfect weather to start a journey. The most prolific creators, thinkers, and leaders don't rely on fleeting moments of inspiration; they rely on showing up consistently, regardless of how they feel.

Inspiration isn't a prerequisite for action—it's often the result of action. Start working, even if the first steps feel uninspired or clumsy. Momentum builds as you engage with the task, and what begins as routine effort can evolve into a spark of creativity. The renowned writer *William Faulkner put it succinctly: "I only write when inspiration strikes. Fortunately, it strikes at nine every morning."*

Treat your creative work or goals like a commitment, not an option. Even on uninspired days, progress, however small, lays the foundation for breakthroughs. Remember, inspiration is not a mysterious muse waiting to grace you; it's a partner that shows up when you do.

➢ "I'm Afraid to Fail"

Fear of failure is a universal feeling, one that often stops us before we even begin. But failure, far from being the end, is a natural and necessary part of growth. It's not a reflection of your worth, but a marker of your courage to try. Every successful person has failed—sometimes spectacularly—before achieving greatness.

The key is to reframe failure. Instead of seeing it as a setback, view it as feedback. Each failure teaches you something valuable—about your strategies, your strengths, and the areas where you can improve. *As Thomas Edison famously said, "I have not failed. I've just found 10,000 ways that won't work."* His persistence reminds us that failure is a step on the path to success.

When fear of failure looms large, ask yourself: What's the worst that can happen? Most of the time, the consequences are not as dire as we imagine. And even if you stumble, you'll gain the resilience, knowledge, and grit needed to tackle the next challenge with confidence. Remember, failure is not the opposite of success – but often its most valuable precursor.

- **"I Get Distracted Easily"**

In today's fast-paced world filled with endless notifications, multitasking demands, and digital temptations, getting distracted is a common challenge. But distractions aren't just external - they often stem from within. Unclear priorities, fatigue, or a wandering mind can pull us away from what truly matters.

The key to overcoming distractions is to regain control of your focus. Start by identifying your biggest time-wasters. Is it scrolling through social media, constantly checking emails, or tackling low-priority tasks? Once you're aware, create boundaries—turn off notifications, set specific work times, or designate "distraction-free" zones.

Building focus is like strengthening a muscle. Begin with small intervals of undisturbed work, such as the Pomodoro Technique: 25 minutes of focused effort followed by a 5-minute break. Gradually increase the time as your ability to concentrate improves.

Remember, focus isn't about eliminating every distraction—it's about learning to prioritize what deserves your attention. When you commit to being intentional with your time, you'll find that distractions lose their power, and your productivity soars.

9. The Role of Purpose in Creativity and Discipline

Purpose is the invisible thread that ties creativity and discipline together. It acts as a guiding star, ensuring that your creative efforts have direction and your disciplined actions are aligned with meaningful goals. Without purpose, creativity can become aimless, and discipline can feel like an exhausting grind. But when both are anchored in a strong sense of purpose, they gain clarity, energy, and impact.

Purpose acts as a Compass. It provides a sense of "why" behind what we do. It answers critical questions: Why am I pursuing this goal? Why does it matter to me? A strong sense of purpose motivates you to persist during challenging times, fuelling both the curiosity of creativity and the perseverance of discipline.

Imagine an artist creating a painting without any emotional connection to the work. The result may be technically proficient but lack soul. Now think of an artist painting to raise awareness for a cause they deeply believe in—every brushstroke carries meaning, and their passion becomes evident in the final piece.

Similarly, purpose energizes discipline. Instead of feeling like an obligation, disciplined habits become empowering steps toward fulfilling your mission. A student studying late into the night to achieve their dream of becoming a doctor isn't simply "following rules"—they're investing in a future aligned with their purpose.

Purpose Provides Boundaries for Creativity

While creativity thrives on freedom, too much freedom can lead to overwhelming options and lack of focus. Purpose acts as a filter, narrowing down possibilities to those that align with your goals and values. It ensures that your creative energy is spent on meaningful ideas rather than scattered efforts.

For instance, a startup founder brainstorming new products might have countless ideas. Without a clear purpose—such as solving a specific problem for their customers—they risk wasting time on innovations that lack relevance or impact.

Purpose Gives Discipline a Context

Discipline without purpose can feel robotic and uninspired. Purpose adds context, reminding you why the effort is worth it. Athletes training rigorously for the Olympics don't just follow routines for the sake of discipline. Their purpose - a shot at representing their country and achieving personal excellence - drives every practice session.

PurposeFuelsResilienceinBothCreativityandDiscipline. Creativity often involves taking risks, experimenting, and failing. Discipline, on the other hand, requires consistency, even in the face of setbacks. Both can be exhausting without a clear sense of purpose to keep you grounded.

Overcoming Creative Block

Purpose acts as a wellspring of inspiration during moments of creative stagnation. When you feel stuck, reconnecting with your "why" can reignite your passion. Ask yourself: What impact am I trying to create? Who am I trying to serve?

A writer experiencing writer's block might rediscover their flow by remembering their purpose: sharing a story that inspires readers to overcome their own challenges.

Sustaining Discipline Through Challenges

Purpose transforms hard work into meaningful effort. When setbacks occur, it's easier to stay disciplined if you're deeply connected to your goals. Think of scientists working on long-term research projects. Despite years of trial and error, their purpose—solving critical problems like curing diseases or addressing climate change—keeps them focused and determined.

Maya Angelou's work as a poet, author, and activist was grounded in her purpose: to uplift marginalized voices and celebrate the resilience of the human spirit. Her creative writing was disciplined, often following structured routines to ensure consistency. This combination allowed her to produce timeless works that continue to inspire generations.

10. Aligning Purpose, Creativity, and Discipline in Your Life

I. **Identify Your Core Purpose**: Your purpose doesn't have to be grand or world-changing—it just needs to resonate deeply with you. Start by reflecting on what excites you, what problems you feel called to solve, or what legacy you want to leave.

Questions to Ask Yourself:

What activities make me lose track of time?

What problems anger or inspire me?

What would I want to be remembered for?

II. **Connect Purpose to Daily Actions**: Once you've identified your purpose, integrate it into your creative and disciplined practices. For example, if your purpose is to improve mental health awareness, ensure that your creative projects and disciplined habits—like maintaining a blog or conducting workshops—align with this mission.

III. **Revisit Your Purpose Regularly**: Purpose isn't static. It evolves as you grow and encounter new experiences. Regularly reassess your purpose to ensure it remains relevant and motivating. Journaling, vision boards, or quiet reflection can help you stay connected to your "why."

IV. **Practical Exercises to Harness Purpose**

The "Purpose Pyramid" Exercise:

- Write down your ultimate life purpose at the top of a pyramid.
- Break it down into smaller goals that support this purpose in the middle layers.
- Identify daily habits and actions that align with these goals at the base.

This exercise helps connect big-picture purpose with everyday actions.

V. **Purpose-Focused Brainstorming**: Before starting a creative project, take 5 minutes to write down how it aligns with your purpose. This clarity will guide your creative choices and ensure that your work remains meaningful.

VI. **Visualize Your Purpose in Action**: Spend time imagining what success looks like when your purpose is fulfilled. How will it impact others? How will it make you feel? This visualization can motivate you during both creative slumps and disciplined routines.

A Powerful Synergy

Discipline and creativity are not opposites—they are allies. When integrated, they create a powerful synergy that allows you to dream big and execute those dreams with precision. By embracing structure without losing flexibility, by staying persistent in the face of challenges, and by always aligning your actions with purpose, you can unlock your full potential.

Remember, the world's most innovative minds—whether scientists, artists, or entrepreneurs—achieved greatness not by chance, but by combining disciplined effort with bold imagination. As you move forward, ask yourself: How can I bring discipline into my creative pursuits? How can I use creativity to make my disciplined efforts more impactful?

By finding the harmony between these forces, you are not just building a life of disciplined purpose—you are creating a masterpiece.

When you align with your purpose, the path forward becomes less about effort and more about flow

Chapter 14

Celebrating Progress and Refining Goals

True success isn't achieved overnight—it's a journey marked by milestones that define, challenge, and propel us forward. Recognizing progress and refining goals along the way is essential to staying motivated and disciplined. In this chapter we delve into a crucial but often overlooked part of any personal growth journey: acknowledging achievements and recalibrating future aims. This stage is where individuals take stock of their successes, however large or small, and celebrate them meaningfully. Recognizing progress isn't just about self-congratulation; it's an essential component of sustained motivation. By celebrating wins, people not only affirm their capabilities but also reinforce positive behaviours, creating a momentum that makes discipline and goal pursuit easier in the long run.

The second, equally important part, is the need to regularly refine and adapt one's goals. As people progress and grow, their aspirations and perspectives may evolve, and rigid goals may no longer serve their ultimate purpose. Refining goals means thoughtfully adjusting plans to stay aligned with deeper values, changing circumstances, and newfound insights. This chapter guides readers on striking a balance between celebrating achievements and recalibrating objectives to stay on a purposeful, evolving path toward success.

1. The Power of Recognizing Progress

Recognizing progress is a powerful force in personal and professional growth. It fuels motivation, builds confidence, and reminds individuals of their journey's purpose. Acknowledging milestones reinforces one's commitment and strengthens resilience, acting as a psychological reward that reinforces the value of disciplined effort. Progress recognition also keeps the momentum alive, making it easier to handle setbacks or delays.

Celebrating progress isn't just about feeling good; it's about reinforcing habits that drive discipline. Every step forward, no matter how small, is a testament to your commitment to a disciplined life. Acknowledging these moments fuels motivation, deepens confidence, and solidifies progress, making it easier to sustain in the face of setbacks.

Furthermore, it allows for reflection and learning. Each milestone celebrated offers an opportunity to assess what strategies worked and what can be refined. For individuals striving for excellence, this acknowledgment is not just a morale booster but a foundation for sustainable growth. Celebrating achievements, no matter how modest, keeps the focus on the bigger picture, fostering long-term commitment to goals.

An example is Google's "20% time" practice, where employees are encouraged to spend 20% of their work hours on innovative projects beyond their regular tasks. This practice led to breakthroughs like Gmail and Google News. By allowing team members to explore, Google not only celebrated progress but encouraged continuous goal-setting through new projects and creative pursuits. This culture of rewarding progress fosters an environment where disciplined innovation thrives.

Leaders who celebrate team accomplishments, even small ones, see higher engagement and loyalty. Similarly, for entrepreneurs and professionals, the act of honouring achievements becomes a positive feedback loop that helps maintain motivation. In this sense, celebrating progress isn't merely self-indulgent but a deliberate, strategic tool for continuous improvement and goal reinforcement.

In personal growth, recognizing progress can be just as transformative. Imagine an aspiring author who commits to writing 500 words daily. Celebrating each milestone - 5,000 words, 10,000 words - enables the author to appreciate the cumulative power of discipline. This can be applied to any personal goal, whether it's building a fitness habit or learning a new skill.

2. Techniques to Celebrate Progress

Celebrating achievements doesn't need grand gestures; it can be as simple as taking a moment to reflect on your journey or sharing your success with others. Here are practical ways to integrate celebration into your disciplined routine:

I. *Set Mini-Milestones*: Break down large goals into smaller, achievable tasks. Each completed task becomes a reason to celebrate. A software developer may celebrate each completed project phase, such as writing code, debugging, and final testing, to sustain motivation through a long development cycle.

II. *Reflect on Progress*: Keep a journal or digital record to document your achievements. Looking back on completed goals reinforces your journey and makes the progress tangible. Reflecting allows you to see how far you've come, reinforcing the discipline that brought you here.

III. *Reward Yourself Meaningfully*: Rewards should align with your values. For some, a reward might be an afternoon off; for others, it might be investing in a new skill or tool to improve further. Ratan Tata, for instance, consistently reinvested in Tata Group's workforce, offering professional development as a reward, thereby aligning personal growth with company objectives.

IV. Share Achievements: Celebrating progress with others creates a support network that keeps you accountable and motivated. Whether it's with colleagues, family, or a social group, sharing successes can make achievements feel more significant and create a cycle of positive reinforcement.

3. Refining Goals: The Art of Course Correction

While celebrating progress is essential, it's equally crucial to periodically reassess and refine goals. The path to success is rarely linear; life's evolving nature demands flexibility. This process of realignment helps maintain relevance and ensures that goals continue to serve your broader purpose.

Refining goals involves three key principles:

I. Evaluate the Relevance of Your Goals: The most effective goals are those aligned with your personal and professional evolution. For instance, an entrepreneur may start with a goal of financial stability, but as the business grows, the focus might shift toward social impact or sustainability.

II. *Embrace New Insights and Adjust Accordingly*: Learning from each step allows you to build more refined goals. A leader who frequently incorporates feedback from employees or stakeholders is better positioned to set goals that resonate with the entire team, fostering a shared vision of success.

III. *Stay Adaptable*: Change is inevitable, and so should be the flexibility of your goals. In a rapidly evolving business landscape, companies like Zoho Corporation pivoted from software as a service to a fully remote workplace model. The shift was a response to the pandemic, but it also became a strategic alignment, reflecting new priorities around employee well-being and innovation.

4. Practical Techniques to Refine Goals

Refining goals can feel daunting, especially if it means revisiting long-held aspirations. However, using structured approaches can make the process intuitive and purposeful.

I. *Quarterly Goal Audits*: Set aside time every few months to evaluate your goals. Are they still aligned with your long-term vision? Are they realistic given your current circumstances? This quarterly audit can prevent drifting from your purpose while allowing room for adaptability.

II. *SMART-ER Goals*: While the SMART framework (Specific, Measurable, Achievable, Relevant, Time-bound) is widely known, adding "Evaluative" and

"Revisable" dimensions ensures continuous improvement. These additional steps promote flexibility and long-term success by encouraging ongoing assessment and adaptation. Regularly *evaluating* progress helps determine if the initial strategies are effective or if any roadblocks require adjustments. The *reassess* phase then allows for changes in response to new insights, shifting priorities, or evolving circumstances, ensuring that goals remain aligned with both personal growth and external developments.

III. *Embrace Feedback Loops*: In professional environments, feedback loops are powerful tools for refining goals. At Infosys, for instance, regular feedback from employees across all levels helps shape strategic direction, leading to a culture of continuous improvement and alignment. Similarly, individuals can benefit from feedback loops by engaging mentors or peers for regular insights. When integrated into personal and professional growth, feedback loops involve regularly reviewing progress, gathering insights, and making adjustments. This can come from self-reflection, peer input, or performance metrics. Effective feedback loops foster continuous improvement, as individuals or teams can course-correct in real time, addressing any shortcomings and building on strengths.

IV. *Mindfulness in Goal Setting*: Mindfulness brings clarity to our motivations, helping us understand why we pursue specific goals. Mindfulness in goal setting means being fully present and aware when defining and pursuing goals. Instead of rushing through objectives or focusing solely on future outcomes, mindfulness encourages individuals to pay attention to their current actions, feelings, and progress. This approach allows for a more thoughtful alignment between personal values and goals, making each objective feel purposeful. Practicing mindfulness helps individuals to avoid burnout by recognizing when they need to rest, adjust their plans, or refocus. It creates a balance between ambition and self-care, fostering a fulfilling, sustainable approach to achievement.

5. Case Studies of Celebrating Progress and Refining Goals

Nike's Evolution in Corporate Social Responsibility (CSR)

Nike, once under scrutiny for its labour practices in the 1990s, made a major shift toward sustainable and ethical practices, gradually transforming its CSR approach into an industry model. After facing severe criticism and backlash, Nike's leadership focused on setting clear, actionable goals around improving labour conditions, reducing environmental impact, and enhancing transparency in its supply chain. By acknowledging both its strengths and areas for improvement, Nike crafted a long-term vision for corporate responsibility and built clear, measurable goals around it.

Over the years, Nike introduced various initiatives aimed at environmental sustainability, such as its "Move to Zero" campaign, which pledges to work toward zero carbon and zero waste. A significant aspect of Nike's progress was the annual report it began to release on its environmental and social impact, allowing stakeholders to see tangible progress. Internally, this report served as a tool for Nike to refine its CSR strategies, adjust focus areas, and set newer, bolder targets. By celebrating each milestone and analysing its impact, Nike effectively turned initial criticism into a platform for continuous improvement.

Tata Group's Balanced Growth in India and Beyond

The Tata Group, one of India's largest and most respected conglomerates, exemplifies a balance of profit-driven growth and purpose-driven initiatives. Under the leadership of the late Ratan Tata and subsequent executives, Tata has prioritized long-term objectives rooted in social responsibility and ethical business practices, rather than just short-term profits. This is seen across its multiple subsidiaries, where Tata continuously refines goals to adapt to the social, economic, and environmental needs of different regions.

Tata Consultancy Services (TCS) consistently sets refined goals for local employment and community investment, providing job opportunities and skills training across India. Tata Motors, another flagship entity, has celebrated progress in environmental responsibility by developing electric vehicles and promoting sustainable mobility. Through regular assessments and feedback loops within its businesses, the Tata Group reinforces its commitment to corporate responsibility, honouring achievements while continuously evolving its strategies to reflect new global challenges. This deliberate attention to progress allows Tata to create impactful changes that align with its longstanding mission of nation-building and social contribution.

Unilever's Sustainable Living Plan

Unilever's Sustainable Living Plan (USLP), launched in 2010, is a prime example of a large corporation aiming to integrate social responsibility directly into its business model. Recognizing the need to address pressing environmental and social issues, Unilever set ambitious targets to reduce its environmental impact and increase positive social outcomes through its brands. The USLP had three primary goals: improving health and well-being, reducing environmental footprint, and enhancing livelihoods for millions.

Unilever's leadership refined these goals periodically to reflect changing priorities and challenges. For instance, as environmental concerns evolved, the company introduced new goals around plastic use and sustainable sourcing. Regular reporting and public accountability became central to Unilever's strategy, as each target was assessed annually and successes celebrated to inspire further commitment. By openly sharing its progress and refining goals over time, Unilever demonstrated how businesses could engage in sustainable practices while driving profitable growth. Through USLP's success, Unilever not only built brand loyalty but also set new benchmarks for corporate responsibility in the consumer goods sector.

6. Personal Growth Through Reflection and Re-commitment

Personal growth is a journey, and at its core, reflection, and re-commitment serve as essential tools to deepen self-awareness and refine goals. Reflection encourages us to pause and evaluate our experiences, achievements, and setbacks, helping us understand what actions brought us closer to our purpose and which habits held us back. When we reflect thoughtfully, we gain clarity, uncovering insights about our motivations, patterns, and personal values. This step becomes a form of self-assessment, allowing us to celebrate our progress, learn from our experiences, and identify new areas for improvement.

Re-commitment, on the other hand, is the active process of using these insights to realign ourselves with our goals. It's not merely about reaffirming previous commitments but about approaching them with a renewed perspective and a refined strategy. After honest reflection, re-commitment brings focus and renewed energy, which is particularly important when we face obstacles or periods of low motivation. Re-commitment is also about flexibility—adjusting our strategies, creating fresh milestones, and adapting to changing circumstances without losing sight of our core objectives.

By engaging in a cycle of reflection and re-commitment, we build resilience and foster a growth mindset. This process can transform setbacks into opportunities, as each experience, whether a success or a failure, becomes a learning tool. Over time, we create a personal growth pathway that is adaptive, purpose-driven, and aligned with both immediate and long-term aspirations. In essence, growth through reflection and re-commitment is a practice of continuous improvement that grounds us in purpose, cultivates mental resilience, and ensures we remain actively engaged with our evolving journey toward self-fulfilment.

Take the example of a young professional working towards a promotion. At each milestone—completing projects, gaining skills, receiving feedback—she has a choice: celebrate these wins and refine her vision for the future or continue working without pause, risking burnout. By valuing each step and adjusting goals based on new insights, she builds not only her career but also a disciplined approach to life.

7. Practical Exercises for Celebrating and Refining Goals

Here are some practical exercises to help you celebrate and refine your goals consistently:

I. Weekly Reflection Ritual: Dedicate 10–15 minutes each week to reflect on your achievements. Note down even minor successes, as they are steps toward your bigger goals. These rituals build gratitude and a positive association with disciplined efforts.

II. *Quarterly Goal Redefinition*: Every three months, assess your long-term goals. Reflect on what's working and what might need adjustment. Write down new insights, experiences, or challenges that could impact your objectives.

III. *Visualization Exercises*: Visualizing future successes and the steps to get there helps reinforce commitment. Each time you celebrate a small win, visualize how it brings you closer to your ultimate goal.

IV. *Creating a Personal Success Map*: Document your journey with a success map. This could be a flowchart, mind map, or timeline, showing each completed milestone and new direction. A success map provides a visual reminder of progress and motivates you to continue moving forward.

It's important to recognize that celebrating progress and refining goals is not a one-time event but an ongoing cycle. Success is not solely defined by the achievement of the final goal, but by the growth, resilience, and learning you experience along the way. Each milestone, whether big or small, represents your commitment, discipline, and perseverance, and deserves to be acknowledged.

Celebrating progress is not about complacency, but about reinforcing the positive momentum that keeps you moving forward. It's about giving yourself the credit you deserve for the hard work and dedication that have brought you this far. This celebration fuels your passion and reminds you of why you started in the first place.

At the same time, it's crucial to remain open to refinement. As you evolve, so too should your goals. Refining your goals doesn't mean abandoning your purpose; it means adjusting your course as new insights, challenges, and opportunities emerge. By constantly reevaluating where you are and where you want to go, you ensure that your journey remains dynamic, relevant, and aligned with your evolving aspirations.

Remember, the pursuit of meaningful goals is not a race, but a journey. Enjoy the process, celebrate the wins, and always be ready to refine your path to align with your highest vision. Keep progressing with purpose and discipline, knowing that each step, no matter how small, brings you closer to becoming the person you're meant to be.

Discipline is the silent architect of greatness, building success one habit at a time

Chapter 15

Living with Disciplined Purpose: A Holistic Approach

Living with a disciplined purpose is about weaving a mindset of intentional action into every aspect of life. For aspiring leaders, entrepreneurs, and anyone pursuing growth, it means anchoring each decision, habit, and ambition in purpose. Success requires more than sheer ambition; it needs thoughtful, disciplined consistency that permeates both personal and professional life.

Living with purpose means aligning actions, values, and goals while cultivating habits that support this alignment over time. A holistic approach to disciplined purpose combines self-awareness, mental clarity, physical well-being, and emotional resilience. The journey requires self-reflection, mindful planning, and continual refinement to adapt to changing circumstances.

1. Finding and Defining Your Purpose

Purpose is the "why" that fuels our journey, helping us steer through challenges and refocus when life becomes chaotic. Each person's purpose is unique and often evolves over time. Defining one's purpose demands introspection, but it doesn't necessarily mean making grand gestures or setting lofty goals; it's about understanding what truly matters.

To gain more clarity, you may consider these introspective practices:

I. *Reflect on Core Values*: Identify the principles you cherish most, such as integrity, innovation, or compassion. Understanding these values makes it easier to set boundaries, choose meaningful pursuits, and navigate distractions.

II. *Evaluate Your Strengths and Passions:* Think about the activities that energize you. For instance, if a young entrepreneur is passionate about sustainability, they might focus on building environmentally conscious businesses.

III. *Consider Your Impact*: Purpose often extends beyond personal gain; it's about contributing to others or the larger world. For instance, companies like Tata Group in India emphasize socially responsible projects, ensuring that their work aligns with broader social goals. On an individual level, this could mean choosing a career or project that positively affects others.

By knowing what you stand for, you can align daily choices with long-term aspirations, creating a life that resonates with meaning and direction.

2. Discipline as a Means of Purpose

Once purpose is defined, discipline becomes the vehicle that propels us toward it. Discipline may seem rigid, but it's the guiding force that helps us stick to our intentions. A disciplined professional, for example, who values family might intentionally carve out daily family time, reinforcing the value they place on relationships.

3. Implementing Purpose-Driven Discipline:

I. *Set Intentional Boundaries*: Boundaries are not restrictions; they're commitments to your purpose. An entrepreneur, for instance, may decide to focus solely on sustainable products and refuse lucrative projects that conflict with this ethos.

II. *Create Non-Negotiable Habits*: Identify daily or weekly habits essential to your goals. Whether it's journaling each morning or spending Sundays on self-care, consistent habits reinforce your dedication to purpose.

III. *Leverage Technology Mindfully*: Use tools that help manage your time without overwhelming your schedule. Apps for meditation, task management, or habit tracking can support a purposeful, disciplined lifestyle.

Purposeful discipline requires a willingness to say "no" to things that don't serve your path. Apple's late co-founder Steve Jobs famously believed in focusing on a few meaningful projects rather than scattering resources across multiple ventures. This focus allowed Apple to deliver innovative, high-quality products, demonstrating the power of disciplined purpose.

4. Nurturing Physical Well-being for Sustainable Discipline

Living with purpose requires a sound body, as physical health is foundational to sustaining energy, clarity, and resilience. Research consistently links physical well-being with improved cognitive function, mood, and overall resilience.

I. *Prioritize Physical Health*: Physical fitness fuels resilience, helping you stay focused and energized. Consider leaders like Virgin Group's Richard Branson, who credits his productivity to daily exercise.

II. *Balance Nutrition and Mental Energy*: Fuel your body with foods that sustain energy and clarity. Avoid extremes, instead focusing on balanced meals that maintain stamina for work and personal pursuits.

III. Practice Restorative Rest: Physical rest is as crucial as productivity, and effective leaders know this. Studies on top CEOs highlight the importance of quality sleep for decision-making and creativity. Allow time for rest to renew both body and mind, creating a disciplined routine that incorporates physical wellness.

Many leaders incorporate yoga and meditation, ancient practices that nurture both body and mind. This holistic approach aligns with the principle of disciplined purpose, proving that true success combines ambition with self-care.

5. Emotional Resilience and Purposeful Living

Discipline without emotional resilience can quickly lead to burnout. Resilience helps us bounce back, maintain a positive outlook, and navigate challenges. Emotional intelligence—the ability to understand and manage emotions—enables disciplined, purpose-driven living.

Building Emotional Resilience:

I. Mindfulness Practices: Mindfulness brings awareness to the present moment, allowing us to respond to challenges without overreaction. Google, for example, encourages its employees to engage in mindfulness programs, knowing it helps with focus, collaboration, and stress management.

II. Journaling for Self-Awareness: Documenting daily thoughts and feelings can provide insight into behavioural patterns and help regulate responses. Regular journaling also reinforces purpose, making it easier to stay aligned with core values.

III. *Engaging in Positive Self-talk*: Developing a practice of positive self-talk can shift mindsets during challenging situations. Whether it's affirming self-worth or reminding oneself of past achievements, this mental discipline bolsters resilience.

Emotional resilience doesn't mean avoiding hardship; it means developing the strength to continue in alignment with purpose, even when challenges arise. Leaders with high emotional resilience remain connected to their purpose, making choices that align with their values rather than succumbing to momentary pressures.

6. Cultivating Purposeful Relationships

Living with a disciplined purpose also involves fostering relationships that support and enrich your journey. For leaders, entrepreneurs, and professionals, relationships are often the foundation of success. Relationships built on trust, respect, and shared values are more likely to sustain under pressure.

Building Strong, Purposeful Connections:

I. *Prioritize Authenticity in Communication*: Open, honest communication fosters stronger bonds, creating supportive networks. Leaders like Satya Nadella at Microsoft are known for their transparent communication, which helps employees align with the company's values and goals.

II. *Seek Out Mentorship and Peer Support*: Learning from others who share similar values can offer guidance and motivation. Consider forming accountability partnerships that reinforce discipline by holding one another to purpose-driven goals.

III. *Give Back to Your Network*: Being a resource for others in your network creates reciprocal support. By offering mentorship, insight, or resources, you build a network that thrives on collaboration and purpose.

Purposeful relationships amplify resilience, keep you grounded, and provide motivation during difficult times. They act as a feedback loop, reinforcing your purpose by surrounding you with people who understand and support your vision.

7. Financial Health and Disciplined Purpose

Financial stability is essential for reducing stress and maintaining focus. Financially disciplined individuals can make choices aligned with purpose without the burden of financial worry. Whether you're building a business, planning a family, or investing in self-improvement, financial health is foundational.

I. *Develop a Purpose-Driven Budget*: A budget aligned with your goals helps avoid unnecessary expenses, directing resources toward what truly matters. Allocate spending that supports growth—like educational resources or health investments—rather than fleeting desires.

II. *Set Long-Term Financial Goals*: Purposeful goals, like saving for personal growth initiatives or supporting meaningful causes, reinforce discipline. Leaders like Warren Buffet advocate for long-term investing, prioritizing disciplined growth over quick gains.

III. *Practice Minimalism*: Minimalism isn't about restriction; it's about prioritizing essentials. Leaders across the globe embrace minimalism to keep focus on goals, avoiding distractions that don't add value.

Financial discipline allows freedom, enabling choices that align with your purpose and reducing anxieties that stem from financial insecurity.

8. A Lifelong Commitment to Disciplined Purpose

Living with a disciplined purpose is a continuous journey, evolving as you grow and adapt. It's not about a single achievement but about the sustained practice of aligning actions with values over time. Staying on this path requires flexibility, openness to learning, and adaptability. It is about creating a life aligned with your deepest values, and consistently making choices that serve those values. It's about building resilience, nurturing relationships, maintaining well-being, and achieving financial stability—all in service of your unique path.

Embrace each day with purpose, making disciplined choices that keep you aligned with your goals and values. Discipline, purpose, and growth work together, creating a life of enduring impact and fulfilment.

In discipline lies the power to rise above distractions and focus on what truly matters

Revisiting the Blueprint

Key Principles and Practices

Purpose as the Guiding Star

Purpose is more than a single goal; it's the overarching reason that fuels our journey. Through self-reflection, identifying your core purpose means connecting with a deeper meaning that inspires every decision, even in moments of uncertainty. Purpose is not static; as you grow, so too will your sense of direction, adapting and deepening with time. Living by purpose is a declaration of your values and the kind of legacy you wish to build.

Discipline as a Steadying Force

While purpose offers direction, discipline is the mechanism that moves you forward. Discipline doesn't confine; rather, it frees you to focus on what truly matters, releasing the distractions and temptations that drain energy. The practices of discipline discussed throughout this book—from time management and goal setting to emotional resilience—serve as reminders that small, consistent actions can create lasting change.

The Power of Resilience and Adaptability

In any purposeful journey, challenges will arise. Resilience allows you to withstand setbacks without losing sight of your goals, while adaptability lets you adjust your approach to meet changing circumstances. Both qualities are essential for sustained growth. When coupled with discipline, they empower you to move forward with confidence, viewing obstacles as opportunities to learn and grow.

A Holistic Approach to Success

The success that endures is comprehensive, touching all aspects of life. True purpose-driven achievement considers physical health, mental clarity, meaningful relationships, and financial stability. By nurturing each area, you create a balanced foundation that supports and sustains your goals. Purpose without health or relationships without emotional growth can feel hollow. Integrating these facets harmonizes your life, grounding you in a well-rounded and deeply fulfilling pursuit.

Call to Action

In our ever-evolving world, the need for disciplined, purpose-driven leaders is vital. As you internalize these principles, consider how you can apply them not only to your personal aspirations but also to influence others positively. The best leaders inspire by example, showing that discipline, resilience, and integrity are essential for navigating complexity. By embracing a disciplined purpose, you also serve as a model for others, sparking the potential within them to lead purposefully.

Taking Ownership of Your Journey

This journey begins and ends with you. The frameworks in this book are tools, but the power to implement them lies in your hands. Reflect on the lessons learned, return to them regularly, and use them to carve a path that is uniquely yours. The journey of disciplined purpose is about committing to the process, staying present, and taking intentional steps—no matter how small—toward the life you envision.

Encouraging Lifelong Learning and Adaptation

In a world marked by rapid change, the leaders who thrive are those who remain open to new ideas, willing to adapt, and committed to continual self-improvement. Recognize that disciplined purpose is a dynamic process. Allow yourself the flexibility to adjust your goals, learn from setbacks, and celebrate progress, no matter how incremental. Lifelong learning is not merely an advantage but a necessity.

Enduring Qualities of Great Leadership in a Complex World

The qualities of purpose-driven leadership remain timeless. As you move forward, remember that true impact lies not in grand gestures but in consistent actions. A disciplined leader with purpose doesn't need to seek the spotlight; their work and commitment speak volumes. Their legacy is not in personal accolades but in the lives they touch, the teams they inspire, and the positive changes they bring about.

As you conclude this journey and step forward, hold these qualities close. You have the blueprint. Now, with discipline, purpose, and resilience as your guides, begin to craft a life that resonates with meaning and purpose—one deliberate step at a time. Your journey has just begun, and the potential within you is boundless.

About the Author

Amit is an Army veteran, a Human Resource Professional, a Coach, a Leadership Trainer, and an Organization Development Consultant. He runs an organization called **Executive Excellence** – *Enabling People & Organizations*. He has been conferred with the coveted "Indian Achiever's Award in HR". With over 30 years of experience, Amit has worked and led HR functions in renowned brands including Clarks Group, Airtel, Ericsson, Tata, TV18 Home Shopping Network, and Formidium Inc.

Amit is a certified ICF and Marshall Goldsmith Stakeholder Centred Leadership Coach and has coached and trained young entrepreneurs, CEOs, CXOs, and senior management professionals from diverse sectors including Retail, Logistics, Banking, and NGOs. Additionally, he has been actively involved in Management Committee Forums and served as a strategic advisor to CEOs. Amit has a keen interest in and knowledge of "TEAL Organizations".

Amit is also passionate about adventure sports, travelling, wildlife photography, cooking, and reading.

Acknowledgment

This book is the culmination of countless lessons learned and experiences shared, and I am deeply indebted to those who have guided, inspired, and supported me along the way.

First and foremost, I extend my heartfelt gratitude to Brigadier Anil Jaithalia, my first mentor and leadership coach. His wisdom, discipline, and encouragement laid the foundation for my journey toward purposeful living and professional growth.

In the corporate world, I have been fortunate to work under exceptional leaders who shaped my perspective and honed my skills. My sincere thanks to Rakesh Kher, S. Vardharajan, Nagakumar, Sandeep Malhotra, and Sanjeev Agrawal for their invaluable mentorship and guidance.

I also want to acknowledge the incredible support and camaraderie of Atul, Jaspreet, Hari, Anshul, Anirudha, Tina, and countless other colleagues and friends who have enriched my journey with their insights, encouragement, and belief in my vision.

To all who have walked this path with me, thank you for your trust, wisdom, and unwavering support. This book is as much a testament to your influence as it is to my own efforts.

www.ingramcontent.com/pod-product-compliance
Lightning Source LLC
LaVergne TN
LVHW091259150826
845673LV00006B/1479

* 9 7 9 8 8 9 6 3 2 4 3 8 6 *